JIM THORPE

Other titles in the **Americans—The Spirit of a Nation** series:

ABRAHAM LINCOLN

"This Nation Shall Have a New Birth of Freedom"

ISBN-13: 978-0-7660-3170-8
ISBN-10:   0-7660-3170-5

CLARA BARTON

"Face Danger, But Never Fear It"

ISBN-13: 978-0-7660-3024-4
ISBN-10:   0-7660-3024-5

EDGAR ALLAN POE

"Deep Into That Darkness Peering"

ISBN-13: 978-0-7660-3020-6
ISBN-10:   0-7660-3020-2

FREDERICK DOUGLASS

"Truth Is of No Color"

ISBN-13: 978-0-7660-3025-1
ISBN-10:   0-7660-3025-3

MATHEW BRADY

"The Camera Is the Eye of History"

ISBN-13: 978-0-7660-3023-7
ISBN-10:   0-7660-3023-7

JIM THORPE

"There's No Such Thing as 'Can't'"

Michael A. Schuman

Enslow Publishers, Inc.
40 Industrial Road
Box 398
Berkeley Heights, NJ 07922
USA

http://www.enslow.com

Acknowledgments

Many thanks to Grace Thorpe and Jack Thorpe for their time and memories of life with their father. I also want to thank Kent Stephens for sharing his knowledge of the intricacies of the early days of college football. Finally, I wish to thank the staffs at the Mason Library at Keene State College and the Keene, New Hampshire, Public Library for their expertise and service.

Library of Congress Cataloging-in-Publication Data

Schuman, Michael.
    Jim Thorpe: "There's no such thing as 'can't'" / Michael A. Schuman.
        p. cm.—(Americans: the spirit of a nation)
    Includes bibliographical references and index.
    Summary: "Explores the life of world class athlete Jim Thorpe, including his
        childhood and American Indian background, his amateur and professional
        athletic career, and the legacy he left behind"—Provided by publisher.
    ISBN-13: 978-0-7660-3021-3
    ISBN-10: 0-7660-3021-0
    1. Thorpe, Jim, 1887–1953—Juvenile literature. 2. Athletes—United States—
        Biography—Juvenile literature. 3. Indian athletes—United States—
        Biography—Juvenile literature. I. Title.
    GV697.T5S45 2009
    796.092—dc22   [B]
                       2008021486

Printed in the United States of America

10 9 8 7 6 5 4 3 2 1

Illustration Credits: Associated Press, pp. 92, 94, 98, 106, 109; Courtesy of Cumberland County Historical Society, pp. 3, 24, 33, 34, 37, 44, 58, 63, 75; Enslow Publishers, Inc., p. 15; Everett Collection, p. 103; Getty Images, pp. 10, 69; Library of Congress, pp. 12, 20–21, 22, 30, 39, 49, 52, 60, 72, 82, 83, 84; NFL, pp. 78, 89; Roger-Viollet / The Image Works, pp. 6, 71; © Shutterstock.com®, pp. 90, 107.

Cover Illustration: Library of Congress (Jim Thorpe in New York Giants baseball uniform).

CONTENTS

Jim Thorpe performs the high jump during the 1912 Olympic Games.

1

Fit for a King

N ot every athlete could become the greatest athlete in the world. But the setting was right for Jim Thorpe.

Thorpe was in Stockholm, Sweden, for the 1912 Summer Olympics. He had already won the gold medal in a track and field competition called the pentathlon, which consists of five events. Thorpe's next test had twice as many events as the pentathlon. The decathlon includes ten events taking place over three days. Only the most skilled and versatile athletes succeed in this challenging contest.

Thorpe had the talent, but he was also determined to prove himself. Thorpe was from the Sac and Fox Nation of American Indians. In 1912, the defeat of American Indians at the hands of the U.S. military was recent history. Although Thorpe's

The Sac and Fox Nation

The Sac and Fox were once two different tribes: the Asakiwaki (Sauk) and Meshkwahkihaki (Fox). Asakiwaki means "people of the yellow earth," and Meshkwahkihaki means "people of the red earth." Both groups lived in the northeastern United States. Settlement by Europeans forced the Sauk and the Fox to move west. Sauk became known as "Sac." Ultimately the groups united in Oklahoma as the Sac and Fox Nation.

The Sac and Fox have lost much of their original way of life. For example, missionaries brought Christianity to the Sac and Fox in an effort to "civilize" them. However, the Sac and Fox Nation mixes Christian religious practices with their traditional religious customs.

father was dead, Thorpe always remembered his words: "Son, you are an Indian. I want you to show other races what an Indian can do."[1]

The decathlon did not start out promising for Thorpe. The weather was not good for the first event, the 100-meter dash. The clouds opened up on the first day, July 13. It poured and poured, turning the track into mud soup. Thorpe never ran well on a sloppy track.

He could usually run the 100-meter dash in 10 seconds. But that day, it took him 11.2 seconds. Thorpe finished second to another American, Eugene Mercer.

The second event was the running broad jump. Conditions were so bad that Thorpe had trouble planting his feet squarely on the takeoff board. If an athlete stepped over the starting line, he received a penalty called a fault. Three faults disqualified a competitor from the competition.

Thorpe faulted on his first try. When he stepped up for his second try, he faulted again. But on his third attempt, Thorpe leaped 22 feet, 2.3 inches. It disappointed him to get third place. Yet it was better than triple faulting.

Thorpe then went indoors to change into a dry tracksuit. He won the third event: the shot put. He put, or pushed in a heaving motion, the 16-pound metal ball 42 feet 5.45 inches. He was now leading the pack in the decathlon after three events.

The weather cleared overnight, and the field was dry on July 14. Under a sunny sky, Thorpe flew over the bar to win the fourth event, the high jump, at 6 feet 1.6 inches. Thorpe's nemesis from the 100-meter dash, Eugene Mercer, won the fifth event: the 400-meter run. In that race, Thorpe finished in fourth place. He made up for that showing in the sixth event: the 110-meter hurdles. Thorpe overpowered his competition and came in first, completing the course in 15.6 seconds. It was a remarkable time for that day.

The final four decathlon events took place on the third day. Thorpe's weakest event was the pole vault.

Jim Thorpe competes in the shot put portion of the decathlon at the 1912 Olympic Games.

Most strong vaulters were lean and wiry. Thorpe was a muscular and barrel-chested two hundred pounder. Big men like Thorpe had broken poles attempting the vault. This time he broke neither the pole nor any record. He landed in third place, clearing the bar at 10 feet 3 inches.

The eighth and ninth events, the discus and javelin throws, call for arm strength. Thorpe finished third in the discus and fourth in the javelin. The final event was the 1,500-meter race. Some observers thought that after winning the pentathlon and participating in nine decathlon events, Thorpe was too tired to win the 1,500. Many of the athletes had already dropped out of the decathlon competition. If Thorpe was tired, it did not show. He finished the race in first place with a time of 4 minutes 40.1 seconds. His closest challenger, Sweden's Gösta Holmér, was almost two seconds behind him.

Each decathlon event is worth a certain number of points. When the final results were tallied, Thorpe had handily won the gold medal. In fact, he had been the frontrunner since he took the lead after the third event. Silver medalist Hugo Wieslander of Sweden was far behind.

Sweden's King Gustav V hosted the medal ceremony. As Thorpe approached the podium, a chorus of cheers erupted from the audience. First, Thorpe received his medal for winning the pentathlon several days earlier.

Then, he was called back to receive his honor for the decathlon. The king placed a laurel wreath on Thorpe's head and handed him his gold medal. Finally, Thorpe was given a silver goblet coated with jewels and formed in the shape of a Viking ship.

Thorpe was about to walk away from the podium when the king grabbed his hand. King Gustav said to Thorpe, "Sir, you are the greatest athlete in the world. I would consider it an honor to shake your hand."[2]

Thorpe was humbled. He replied, "Thanks, King."[3]

2

At Home on the Prairie

Jim Thorpe was born with a twin brother, Charles. As no birth certificate for the Thorpe twins has ever been found, there are different stories about Jim's formal name. It is usually said to be James Francis Thorpe. However, his baptism record lists his name as Jacobus Franciscus Thorpe.

There are also different versions of the twins' birthday. For a long time, it was thought to be May 28, 1888. Historians doing research later learned through baptismal records that the boys

American Indian Reservations

An American Indian reservation is an area of land put aside by the United States government for American Indians. There they live under their own leadership with limited government interference. Reservations were started in the late 1800s after many battles between the United States military and various American Indian nations. The two sides often signed treaties after the fighting had ended. Many treaties allowed for the creation of reservations.

Some Indian reservations today have astounding poverty rates. To help tackle poverty, the leaders of some reservations have built casinos on their land. Gambling is illegal in much of the United States, but is legal on these reservations. The casinos offer entertainment and sporting events. The money tourists spend at the casinos has helped raise the standard of living for many American Indians.

Not all American Indians live on reservations today. Many live in cities and towns throughout the United States.

were born on May 22, 1887, near what is today the town of Prague, Oklahoma.

However, Oklahoma did not become a state until 1907. When Jim and Charlie were born, it was officially called Indian Territory.

Thorpe's parents, Hiram and Charlotte, already had several children. Tragically, most did not survive childhood. Their first child George, born in 1882, was one of the few who lived to be an adult. Jim and Charlie also had an older half brother named Frank.

It was Sac and Fox Indian tradition for a baby's name to reflect an event occurring around the time of his birth. Since the sun was shining on the path to the Thorpe cabin that day, Jim was given the Sac and Fox name Wa-tho-huck. In the language of the Sac and Fox, it means "Bright Path."

Actually, Jim was of mixed ancestry. His mother, who was born Charlotte Vieux, was part French Canadian and part American Indian. His father was part Irish and part American Indian.

A Common Log Cabin

Many American Indians in Indian Territory lived in traditional bark-covered shelters or tepees. The Thorpes, however, lived in a log cabin like those of white settlers. When not at home, Jim and Charlie spent their earliest days picking berries, playing follow the leader, or climbing trees. They competed with each other in wrestling and foot races. Jim almost always won these contests.

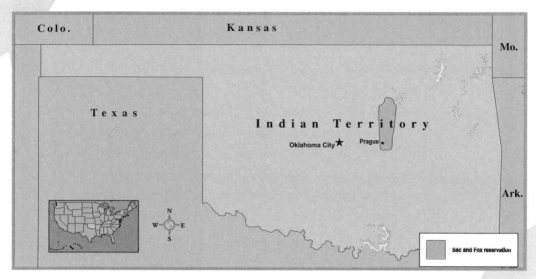

Indian Territory was a portion of land set aside for American Indians to live on. Today, it is the state of Oklahoma.

Jim might have been able to beat his brother, but he felt he was unable to compete against trained athletes. He later said:

> *When I was a kid, I didn't ever expect to get very far in sports. I wasn't big enough for one thing. And the way we lived—way off from everything— made it hard to learn. We didn't have a coach and most of the time we played barefoot. We made our own balls out of whatever was handy, used sticks for bats, flat rocks for bases, and made up our own rules.*[1]

When the twins were young, Hiram taught them how to ride a horse and hunt. The boys also loved to swim and fish in the muddy North Canadian River. Despite the river's name, it is located more than a thousand miles south of Canada and was within walking distance of Jim's cabin.

Jim and Charlie were fraternal twins, which means they were not identical. Charlie had a darker complexion and hair the color of milk chocolate. Jim had a lighter complexion and solid black hair. Despite the twins' differences in appearances, their personalities were similar. Neither boy could get enough of the open air.

Hiram Thorpe was known for being a roughneck, or rowdy person. However, he was also one of the few in the region who could read and write. He thought the best way American Indian children could succeed was through a good education.

Off to School

When the twins were about six-and-a-half years old, Hiram and Charlotte placed them in the closest American Indian school to their home. It was called the Sac and Fox Indian Agency School and was about twenty-five miles away. Automobiles were rare so people traveled mostly on horseback or by horse-drawn wagons. It would take too long for the Thorpe boys to come home from school every day. So they boarded, or lived, in residences near the school.

Historians have viewed the Sac and Fox Indian Agency School as a mixed blessing for American Indians. On one hand, the U.S. government paid for the Indians' education. On the other hand, the school staff had a goal of what they called "civilizing" American Indians. That meant teaching them to adopt the ways of Americans of European background rather than be true to their own heritage.

The Language Problem

The children were punished for speaking their own American Indian languages. The school required them to speak English. They were also not allowed to use their American Indian names. The school assigned English names to those who did not have them. Much of the time these were names of war heroes or presidents. So it was not unusual to see American Indian schoolchildren named George Washington for the first president of the United States or John Brown for the abolitionist.

Because the Thorpe twins had learned to speak English at home, they had no problem adjusting to the school's language rule. But the school had strict discipline, and Jim had a problem with that. The boys had to make their beds and polish their shoes regularly. They had to wear a suit every day and march in step to class. Teachers often hit the children to punish them.

In their studies, the Thorpe boys reversed roles. Unlike in sports, Jim always seemed to play catch-up with Charlie in the classroom. Jim disliked being cooped up in a dormitory room. He missed the endless prairies and thick forests where he used to play.

Playing the New Game

The part of school Jim liked best was playing baseball. His brother, George, was also a student at the school. George taught Jim the game, and before long Jim played baseball on a makeshift diamond.

However, a tragedy in either late 1896 or early 1897 changed Jim's life forever. A disease spread through the school. Some historians say it was typhoid fever. Others say it was influenza, or the flu. Still others claim it was pneumonia. All three of those diseases now can be cured by antibiotics. However, antibiotics did not exist in the 1890s, and doctors were scarce on the reservation. One student who fell seriously ill was Charlie Thorpe. The teachers tried caring for him as they did with other sick students, but he died shortly afterward.

Life Without Charlie

Almost immediately, Jim became moody and spent a lot of time alone. Without his brother, Jim seemed lost. His only regular companion was a pet dog. Sometimes he camped out overnight on the lonely prairie with only himself and his dog. Jim did not want to return to school. He asked his father if he could stay home and help around the family farm.

Hiram Thorpe insisted that his son return to the Sac and Fox Indian Agency School. Yet being there brought back memories of Charlie. Jim was

Jim did not want to return to school.

miserable. He made little effort to make new friends. He had trouble concentrating on his studies. Not even the prairie baseball games were fun anymore.

One day after breakfast, Jim walked off the school grounds and kept walking. He did not stop until he had reached his family home, twenty-five miles away. Hiram was outraged.[2] He wasted no time returning Jim to school. But as soon as his father left, Jim ran back home. One story goes that Jim took a shortcut along back roads that was only eighteen miles long. By taking that shortcut he arrived home ahead of his father.

Hiram Thorpe was far from pleased to return home and see his son standing there. He firmly told Jim, "This time, I'm going to send you so far away from home you'll never be able to find your way back to the ranch."[3]

Kansas

Hiram sent Jim to Haskell Institute, a school for American Indians in Lawrence, Kansas. It was about 370 miles from the Thorpe home. Haskell was also a government-run school. Jim arrived there on September 17, 1898. The Haskell instructors believed in discipline as much as those at the Sac and Fox Indian Agency School.

Jim's area of study was electrical engineering, a science in its earliest stages. However, Jim was not very interested in academics. He preferred athletics. Haskell's sports teams were among the best in

This photo of the Haskell Institute campus was taken in 1913.

the Midwest. One of Haskell's best athletes was Chauncey Archiquette. Thorpe admired the older and bigger Archiquette, who starred in baseball, basketball, and football. One day Archiquette went up to Jim and chatted with him. Archiquette was stunned to discover how little Jim knew about football.

The Makeshift Football

Archiquette took Jim to the school's harness shop. Jim used machinery there to sew together a makeshift football of old leather stuffed with rags. Although a crude design, the football satisfied Jim. He organized games with other classmates. When Jim proved he could outrun and outplay boys his own age, he began competing against older students.

Jim's dream job was not going to be in electronics. He later said, "I never was content unless I was trying my skill in some game against my fellow playmates or testing my endurance and wits against some member of the animal kingdom."[4]

Jim finally had adjusted to life at Haskell. Then one day in 1901, he received a letter from home. It read that his father had been injured in a hunting accident and was dying. Instead of allowing the school to arrange for time off, Jim merely walked away from the school grounds and headed toward the nearest train tracks. As a freight train chugged by, he ran alongside a boxcar with an open door. He picked up enough speed to hop on board.

A Long Walk Home

Jim Thorpe did not stay on the train for long. He jumped out and started walking. Some say that a

American football was still in its early stages when Jim Thorpe first learned about it.

worker on the train discovered Jim was riding for free and threw him off.

Others say the train was heading north toward Nebraska instead of south to Oklahoma. As soon as Jim discovered he was heading in the wrong direction, he bolted and started walking south. Once in a while he hitched a ride on a horse-drawn wagon for a short distance. About fourteen days after he had left, he reached his family's cabin. After getting off the train, he had traveled about 270 miles, mostly on foot, in those two weeks.[5]

Jim was shocked to see his father was alive and well. It was true that Hiram Thorpe had been shot, but he was not dying. By the time Jim arrived to see him, Hiram was recovering.

Jim never returned to Haskell. He believed he was needed more on the farm than at school. This time, Hiram Thorpe did not force Jim to go back.

Jim spent the summer and fall of 1901 hunting game and tending the family's pigs and cattle. He most enjoyed working with his father's horses. Although Jim was a little under five feet tall and just over one hundred pounds, he was strong and tough. He liked being on his father's ranch, but those happy days were not to last.

That fall, Jim's mother, Charlotte, gave birth to the family's eleventh child, a boy named Henry. The baby lived only a few days. Shortly afterward, on November 17, 1901, Charlotte Thorpe died from complications due to Henry's birth. She was just thirty-nine years old.

Charlotte's death crushed the entire family.[6] They had trouble adjusting to life without a wife and mother. Hiram Thorpe and his children seemed to be constantly at one another's throats. Jim, only fourteen years old, needed a break from his home life.

To the Gridiron

O ne day, Hiram Thorpe went away for several hours and left Jim in charge of the family's livestock. But Jim had fun in mind. He and his brother George went fishing. Hiram Thorpe returned to find his animals roaming all over the farm. When Jim and George came home from their fishing trip, Hiram beat his two boys. Jim ran away from home and settled in the Texas Panhandle where he got a job on a ranch. Part of his responsibility included taming wild horses.

Jim was a skilled horse handler. He learned how to interpret a horse's movements—what different horses meant when they flicked their manes or blinked their eyes a certain way. Sometimes he worked with disagreeable horses. If he misinterpreted what a horse wanted, he was often bitten or kicked. Jim withstood his aches and pains. In time, he earned enough money to buy his own team of horses.

Heading Home

After about a year in Texas, Jim took his horses and returned home. Hiram Thorpe was relieved to see him. He enrolled Jim in nearby Garden Grove School. This was a public school for all children, not just American Indians. It was only three miles away from home, so Jim could help with farm chores when not in school.

While Garden Grove School was not wealthy, its administrator, Walter White, did what he could to provide athletic facilities for the students. He laid out a track for running. He set up poles and bars for the pole vault and high jump. He held a fund-raising dinner so the school could purchase baseball bats and gloves.

To Carlisle

Early in 1904, Jim made a decision that would forever affect his life. He had heard about a school in Carlisle, Pennsylvania. Carlisle Indian Industrial School (CIIS) was founded in 1879 for American Indian children to learn trades and assimilate into non-American Indian culture. Most historians today say the assimilation idea made the school unfair to American Indians. However, in its day many people praised the school for allowing American Indians opportunities they could not get elsewhere.

Hiram Thorpe encouraged Jim to attend Carlisle. He said it was a place Jim could show the world the good things American Indians could do. Jim agreed. His daughter Grace later said that her father had no problem with Carlisle despite the assimilation policy. She noted, "He did not have anything bad to say about the Indian boarding school and he grew up in it."[1] Jim Thorpe's son Jack noted, "At the time he didn't really know the difference. That's what he was used to."[2]

As at Haskell, sports were Thorpe's main interest at Carlisle, which had one of the nation's best football teams. In the early 1900s, football was not the major sport it is now. The National Football League (NFL) did not exist. The only game was college football. Carlisle's coach, Glenn Scobey Warner, was known as one of the best coaches. When Warner played football at Cornell University in Ithaca, New York, he was twenty-five years old. That made him the team's oldest player. Because of that, his teammates gave him the nickname, Pop. Warner later helped found the kids' football organization known today as Pop Warner Football.

On June 1, 1904, Jim arrived in Carlisle. He quickly learned that the school was run like a military academy.

A Strict Life

Jim was referred to as "Cadet Thorpe." All the students had their long hair cut to look more like white Americans. The students marched from class to class in groups. They awoke at 5:30 A.M. and had breakfast together at 6:15. Girl students served breakfast to the boy students.

All students took both academic and vocational classes where they learned trades. Females learned about things such as childcare, dressmaking, and cooking. Males attended blacksmithing, tinning, carpentry, and tailoring classes. There were no classes in electrical engineering, so Jim studied tailoring. The school required all students to attend Sunday church services. Carlisle founder, Richard Henry Pratt, said of the students, "We keep them moving, and they have no time for homesickness—none for mischief—none for regret."[3]

Jim was just getting used to life at Carlisle when he received word that once again tragedy had struck at home. His father had died, most likely of blood poisoning. By the time Jim received the news, Hiram Thorpe's funeral had already taken place.

The "Outing System"

Jim became as depressed as he had after the deaths of his brother and mother. The Carlisle staff had a way to handle such unhappy students. It was called "the outing system." As part of the system, the staff sent Jim off campus to live with a white family. The goal was to keep a student busy while giving him or her a taste of the outside world.

Jim's first white family had him cook and clean the house. Such chores were considered women's work at the time. Jim was unhappy cooking and mopping floors. Shortly afterward, his school sent him to live with another family.

After three months with them, he went to live on a farm in Robbinsville, New Jersey, that belonged to Harby Rozarth. For the next three years, Thorpe spent his days working the fields on Rozarth's farm. He did such a fine job that he was promoted to foreman, or boss, over other American Indian students working there.

When Thorpe returned to Carlisle in the spring of 1907, he was a wiry mass of muscle. The three years of hard farm labor proved to be a superb bodybuilding workout. Still, some members of Carlisle's athletic staff, like trainer Wallace Denny, told Thorpe he was too thin to play football. Denny told Thorpe he would get killed playing the game. Thorpe, now almost twenty years old, stood 5 feet 9.5 inches tall and weighed 144 pounds.[4]

Impressing Carlisle's Athletes

One spring afternoon, when Thorpe walked across the track field, he noticed Carlisle's varsity track team practicing the high jump. Thorpe stopped and watched as the athletes made higher and higher leaps over the bar. But when the bar reached five feet nine inches, none of the team members could top it. The team decided to call it a day, but Thorpe humbly asked if he could try.

Thorpe was not wearing a sports uniform. He had on a pair of overalls and borrowed gym shoes. The varsity athletes looked at Thorpe as if he was crazy. Their attitude changed when he easily cleared the bar. The track team was astonished.

On the Team

A student named Harry Archenbald told Pop Warner about Jim Thorpe's amazing leap. The next day, Thorpe was told to report to Warner's office. Thorpe was convinced he was in trouble for interfering with the track team's practice.

Warner asked Thorpe if he knew why he was there. Thorpe answered that he hoped it was for nothing bad. Warner said it was just the opposite. He told Thorpe he had broken the school's high-jump record. No Carlisle high jumper had ever topped the 5-feet-9-inch mark. Thorpe said he probably could have jumped higher had he been wearing a proper tracksuit. Warner told Thorpe he was now on the track team.

While Thorpe had raw talent, he needed an older and more seasoned student to help him polish his skills. Warner got a twenty-three-year-old star athlete named Albert "Ex" Exendine to assist Thorpe. Exendine and Warner put Thorpe on a tough training program. As a newcomer, Thorpe was hardly a star on the track team, but he did show basic skills.

Jim Thorpe (left) races Thomas McLaughlin (right) of the Loughlin Lyceum in Boston. Thorpe's first experience with sports at Carlisle was as a member of the track team.

Since he was a varsity athlete, Thorpe did not spend the summer with a farm family. Coach Warner's players spent summers with their coach training for the fall sports season. That meant football.

Although football was not as intricate as it is today, one thing was the same. The object was to get the ball across the opponents' goal line. Touchdowns counted for five points. Field goals were four points.[5] There were no specialized separate teams for offense and defense. Each man played both sides. It was common

The Meeting That Saved Football

By today's standards, football in the early 1900s was dangerous. Helmets were made of soft leather and little padding. There were few rules to protect players from serious injury. The rules that existed were rarely enforced. In the 1905 college football season, a total of twenty-three players died due to football injuries.[6] Some colleges had banned football altogether.

President Theodore Roosevelt loved football, but only when it was played cleanly and fairly. He compared football to life. In an article he wrote for a children's magazine, Roosevelt said that, "in life, as in a football game, the principle to follow is: Hit the line hard; don't foul and don't shirk, but hit the line hard!"[7]

Roosevelt was determined to save football. He held a meeting at the White House. Representatives from over sixty colleges attended. One result was the formation of the National Collegiate Athletic Association (NCAA). This is the same group that oversees college sports today.

Another result was a lot of new rules. Previously, a team needed five yards to get a first down. That was changed to ten yards. This meant that players would be spread across a wider area. That, in turn, meant more finesse and less physical contact. Another rule established a neutral zone between the teams at the line of scrimmage.

One rule revolutionized the game. Before the meeting, players could gain yards only by running with the ball. It was decided at the conference to legalize forward passes. They had to be thrown from at least five yards behind the line of scrimmage. They also had to be at least ten yards in distance.

for quarterbacks or other halfbacks to serve as kickers or kick returners.

The Spiral Pass

When Carlisle's players first tried passing, they could not get any distance. Albert Exendine credited Warner with developing the spiral pass to remedy that problem.[8] Although other college coaches had their quarterbacks throwing ten- and fifteen-yard passes, Warner's players threw spiral passes of forty to fifty yards. It was not just the quarterback who passed. Warner expected all his backs to learn how to throw a spiral.

Warner was hesitant to let Thorpe play football right away. The coach saw Thorpe as a future track star and did not want him injured. Thorpe insisted that Warner give him a chance. To keep Thorpe happy, Warner let him practice as a kicker, a position with minimal contact. But Thorpe told the coach he wanted to play a position where he could carry the ball. So Warner decided to teach Thorpe a lesson about the game's toughness.

How Tough Was Thorpe?

During one practice, Warner handed the ball to Thorpe and told him to run with it. His intent was to use Thorpe as tackling practice for the other players. But things did not work out as Warner intended. Thorpe

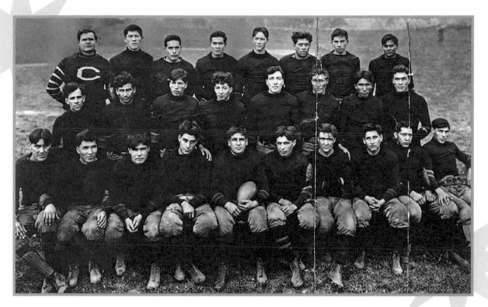

Thorpe (top row, second from left) stands next to his coach, Pop Warner (top row, left), in this picture of the 1907 Carlisle football team.

zigzagged through the defense all the way to the end zone.

Warner gave Thorpe the ball again and demanded that his players use their tackling skills. As Thorpe ran, would-be tacklers bumped off him as if he was made of rubber. Others grabbed him, but Thorpe broke loose from their grips. Again Thorpe made it to the goal line. He then simply handed the football to Warner and said, "Nobody tackle Jim."[9]

Jim Thorpe had proven to Warner that his gridiron skills were too good to waste. Warner said Thorpe could play halfback. The first game of the season was just weeks away.

Shining at Carlisle

J im Thorpe may have been talented, but many teammates had more experience. During the first game of the season on September 21, 1907, Thorpe sat on the bench. The opponent was Lebanon Valley College, a small school. Carlisle crushed them 40–0.

Publicly the Carlisle starting eleven used their English names. Privately many went by their American Indian names. For example, one of the starting ends, Antonio Lobo, used his American Indian name, Wolf. Starting tackle Samuel McClean's American Indian name was Man-Afraid-of-a-Bear.

Some also went by a third name, a nickname based on their most unattractive feature. Kidding each other in a good-natured manner helped the players bond as a team. One young man with big ears was called Mule. One who did not like to bathe was Skunk. A third player was called Dog because his teammates thought he looked like a bulldog. At first, Coach Warner thought Dog was the player's American Indian name. After one play Warner called out, "Good work, Dog."[1] The other players almost fell over laughing.

After Lebanon Valley, Carlisle took on college powerhouses. Most were bigger colleges with more students. Carlisle had about 250 male students old enough to play football.[2] Some opponents had three or four times as many. Therefore, these other schools had a larger pool of men from which to draw players.

A Big Crowd in Buffalo

Thorpe warmed the bench during the Carlisle Indians' next game. It was a hard fought 18–5 victory over bigger, beefier Penn State. Thorpe did not log any time on the field until the third game, against Syracuse in upstate New York. In order to draw as big a crowd as possible, the game was played in the bigger city of Buffalo, New York, about 140 miles west of Syracuse.

The Halfback

The game was aggressive, with injuries resulting on both sides. At one point, Carlisle's starting halfback Albert Payne was hit hard and had to leave the game. Jim Thorpe, so far untested outside of practice, replaced him.

Thorpe was so inexperienced that he did not know most of his team's signals. Quarterback Frank Mt. Pleasant told Thorpe not to worry. He told Thorpe to simply do what he said. When he told Thorpe where to run, Thorpe did so. When he told Thorpe which blockers to follow, Thorpe kept his eye on those blockers and stayed behind them. Thorpe played a solid game, but he did not stand out. He had no breakout runs. But he also had no fumbles and did not get tackled for any losses. Carlisle won 14−6. Thorpe's fellow halfback Pete Hauser scored all fourteen points.

In Carlisle's next game against in-state rival Bucknell, Thorpe replaced the hobbling Payne in the first quarter. He ended up playing most of the game. In a matter of seconds, he almost turned from hero into goat. Thorpe returned a kickoff from deep in Carlisle's own territory to deep into Bucknell's. When a touchdown seemed a sure thing, Thorpe was hit on his blind side by a Bucknell defender. Thorpe fumbled the ball on Bucknell's 10-yard line. The ball dribbled 3 yards forward when Carlisle teammate Theodore Owl picked up the ball and ran it into the end zone. Owl's touchdown saved Thorpe from an embarrassing turnover.

Carlisle won 15−0. In Carlisle's student newspaper, Thorpe's play was mentioned in print for the first time. The article said, "Thorpe did most of the work carrying the ball and proved to be an excellent ground gainer."[3]

Thorpe Learns a Lesson

In the next game against undefeated University of Pennsylvania (Penn), Thorpe learned a valuable lesson about team play. Penn is a member of the Ivy League conference, which one hundred years ago had some of college football's best teams.

Thorpe (right) soon proved himself an asset to the Carlisle team. Above, he holds the ball.

Thorpe did not start, but replaced injured Pete Hauser at halfback early in the first quarter. Thorpe took a handoff from Mt. Pleasant and made a major mistake by not following his blockers. While they went one direction, Thorpe went another. He crashed into a wall of defenders who tackled Thorpe for a loss of yards.

Thorpe learned quickly. The next time he was handed the ball, Thorpe stayed back for a second and watched his blockers. He saw a path open up and followed it 75 yards for his first touchdown.

Carlisle won 26−6. Regional newspapers raved about the team. However, much of the coverage included racial stereotypes of American Indians. The *Philadelphia Press* wrote, "With racial savagery and ferocity, the Carlisle Indian eleven grabbed Pennsylvania's football scalp and dragged their victim up and down Franklin Field."[4] Thorpe was not pleased with write-ups like that. He felt a white team would not have been treated in the same manner.[5]

Another Ivy League college, Princeton University in New Jersey, was next on Carlisle's schedule. Princeton was not as highly regarded as Penn, and Carlisle was expected to win with little trouble. For the first time, Thorpe started. As before, he played halfback.

The teams played at a stadium called the Polo Grounds in New York City. It was the home ballpark for baseball's New York Giants (today the San Francisco Giants). In the future, it would also be home to professional football's New York Giants. The Polo Grounds could seat nearly thirty-nine thousand fans per game.[6]

The Princeton-Carlisle game was played at the Polo Grounds in New York City.

On the day of the Princeton-Carlisle game, it was about 80 percent full. This crowd included some of the wealthiest people in New York City. The men wore their finest suits and fashionable straw hats. Young women dressed in gowns, ribbons, and bows.

Unfortunately, the game turned out to be a total disaster, for both the fans and Carlisle's football team. The weather was horrible. Rain poured down like the

The Polo Grounds

The Polo Grounds was one of the strangest stadiums in professional sports history. Some said it was shaped like a giant bathtub. The ballpark was remodeled several times during its fifty-two years of existence, but the distance between home plate and the center-field wall generally ranged between 480 and 505 feet.[7] Therefore, it was almost impossible to hit a home run to center field. In no major league game did a ball ever hit the center-field clubhouse wall.[8]

The distance down the left-field line ranged between 250 and 280 feet.[9] Down the right-field line, the distance was just 249 to 257 feet.[10] That made for a lot of cheap home runs that would have been weak pop-ups in most other ballparks.

The Polo Grounds was located in the Harlem section of New York City. It sat just across the Harlem River from Yankee Stadium. The ballpark had its unusual shape because polo was once played on that location, although in a different stadium. That first stadium was built with dimensions suited to the game of polo. The last game at the Polo Grounds was played on September 18, 1963. The ballpark was demolished in 1964. An apartment complex is on the site today.

water at Niagara Falls. The fans were drenched, and those who dressed to show off saw their expensive clothes ruined by the driving rain.

As early as the first quarter, the players were covered with mud from their helmets to their shoes. The football field turned into a 100-yard mud pit. Visibility was so poor that receivers had trouble seeing the ball in the air. The final score was 16–0 in favor of Princeton.

Analyzing a Loss

Why did Carlisle lose to a weaker team? Carlisle had been relying all season long on a strong passing game. Their running backs had used speed over sheer power to break away for long gains. Passing and that style of running were nearly impossible in the poor conditions. Princeton was a big, lumbering team that used brute force as opposed to Carlisle's nimble running and pinpoint passing.

On the other hand, some sports historians said that Carlisle might have lost even if the weather had been clear and dry. They said that Carlisle was so thrilled with their win the previous week that they slacked off against Princeton. They may have been looking ahead to their game the following week against another tough opponent, Harvard.

To make matters worse, one of Princeton's favorite anti-Carlisle cheers ended with the words, "Poor Mr. Indian." Thorpe found it insulting.[11]

Stereotypes and Prejudice

Carlisle's starters were all healthy for the Harvard game so Thorpe sat on the bench. There is no record of him entering the game as a substitute. Carlisle made up for their disaster against Princeton and topped Harvard 23–15. Again, stereotypes marred the coverage. *The New York Times* wrote, "Harvard was scalped by the Indians this afternoon in the fastest game seen in the Stadium [sic] this fall."[12]

Although the men from Carlisle did not enjoy being stereotyped in that manner, they could not do much about it. Thorpe's son Jack Thorpe explained:

> *That's the way it was at the time, in the early part of the century. This was not many years after [American Indian] leader Geronimo surrendered [to the U.S. Army]. A lot of the same writers covered Geronimo. The guys [from Carlisle] just lived with it. Here we are in 2008 and we still have to live with a lot of [stereotyping].[13]*

Even worse, numerous hotel owners did not allow American Indians to stay in their buildings. On many occasions, the young men from Carlisle had to go out of their way to find hotels that would admit them. Jack Thorpe said, "They couldn't stay in the big hotels. In fact, they couldn't stay where Coach Warner stayed."[14]

Thorpe started at halfback in Carlisle's next game, against the University of Minnesota. However, when the game got close, Albert Payne replaced him. Carlisle squeaked past Minnesota 12–10. Carlisle also won its last game of the season by beating Big Ten Conference champs the University of Chicago 18−4. As in the Harvard game, Thorpe spent the entire game on the bench.

Carlisle ended the season 10−1. At the time, there were no bowl games. Nor was there any kind of college football championship series. The season simply ended with the last scheduled game.[15] While Thorpe did not excel, he did his part.

In the Classroom

After the season, Thorpe showed the same skill in class that he had on the football field. As he matured, Thorpe took his studies more seriously. In academic subjects, such as arithmetic, grammar, history, and literature, Thorpe received grades of "excellent." In his vocational class, house and carriage painting, he earned a grade of "good."

Thorpe earned respect from younger classmates as both a football player and a student. Some of the younger kids went to him for help, and he enjoyed being a kind of teacher's aide. One day, Thorpe's history teacher asked him to take over the class and teach the students about the Civil War.[16]

Track Season

Still, athletics remained Thorpe's number one interest. Spring 1908 meant track season. Though Thorpe was a fast runner, his best events involved jumping. In a meet against Syracuse on May 14, 1908, Thorpe won both the 120-yard and 220-yard hurdles. While competing against Dickinson College, in Carlisle, Pennsylvania, he won the 220-yard hurdles as well as the high jump, long jump, and high hurdles. He also set a new school record in the shot put. At the State Intercollegiate Meet on May 30, Thorpe finished first in the high jump and second in shot put, low hurdles, and high hurdles.

In 1908, it was hard to make good money playing football. Some midwestern towns had started semipro football teams. However, they were poorly organized and the pay was little, if any. The only sport in which athletes were paid decent wages was baseball.

After track season, Thorpe joined Carlisle's baseball team, which was also coached by Pop Warner. The baseball and track seasons overlapped a bit. By the time Thorpe joined the baseball team, there were only a few games left in the season. His best effort was a 1–0 shutout he pitched against Albright College in Reading, Pennsylvania.

Some of Thorpe's teammates spent the summer playing semiprofessional baseball to earn extra money. Others trained for track and field events for the 1908

Thorpe was ready for the 1908 track season.

Summer Olympics in London. Thorpe did neither. He headed back to Oklahoma.

Back on the Farm

At his family farm, Thorpe spent a lot of time hanging around with his brothers and sisters. He liked to help out his brother Frank on his farm. When not plowing fields, the two brothers fished for bass and catfish.

Jim Thorpe, now twenty-one, returned to Carlisle late that summer. Coach Warner assigned Thorpe the offensive positions of halfback and place-kicker on the football team. When opposing teams had the ball, Thorpe played defensive back. And when Carlisle fell short of a first down, Thorpe was often the punter.

A New Season

The season's first football game was scheduled for September 19, 1908, against Conway Hall, a prep school for Dickinson College. As in the 1907 season, Albert Payne started at halfback. But when Payne was shaken up early on, Thorpe replaced him. Thorpe ran for 5 touchdowns and threw for another. And that was all in the first half! With the game out of reach, Thorpe rested in the second half. Carlisle won 53−0.

In the second game, Carlisle shut out Lebanon Valley 35−0. As against Conway Hall, Thorpe outshined his opponents and was taken out before the second half.

The third game, against Villanova, was expected to be an easy victory. Warner benched Thorpe to rest him for tougher games later on. But Villanova's defense gave Carlisle more than it bargained for. Late in the game, with the score tied 0−0, Warner sent in Thorpe to take charge.

Thorpe took the ball on the first handoff play and crashed into the defensive line. He maneuvered his way around every defender in the backfield and ran 70 yards for a touchdown. It was the play of the game as Carlisle went on to win 10−0.

Against respected Penn State on October 3, Thorpe used his toes to lead Carlisle to victory. He kicked 3 field goals—a field goal was still worth four points—in a 12−5 win.

Tough Opponents

Mighty Syracuse was Carlisle's opponent the next week. Syracuse had outscored its opponents 66−5 in its previous games that season.[17] Again, Thorpe's field-goal kicking took down a powerful opponent. He booted three, accounting for all of Carlisle's points in a 12−0 win. Their next scheduled game, against Susquehanna University, was canceled. That allowed Pop Warner an extra week to rest and train his team.

They would need it for their October 24 game against the University of Pennsylvania. Penn had two All-Americans, including double threat Bill Hollenback. Hollenback was respected as both an efficient quarterback and a feared tackler. Thorpe said of him, ". . . no one was in class with him as a tackler. I could sidestep a lot of others or fake them into making foolish dives. But not Bill. When he came at me, I knew it was just a question of how hard he'd hit me. When he did hit me, it was like being struck by a battering ram."[18]

Penn scored first with a touchdown and extra point for a 6–0 lead. The game then became a defensive struggle, with Carlisle forcing 8 Penn turnovers. In the second half, with the ball on the Penn 40-yard line, Thorpe caught a forward pass. He then scurried past Hollenback and ran the length of the field for a touchdown. Thorpe kicked the extra point. The game ended in a 6–6 tie.

Thorpe said that was the toughest game he played in all his years of football.[19] Late in the game, Thorpe sprained an ankle. Because of the injury, he sat out the next game against Navy. Even without Thorpe, Carlisle won 16–6.

Thorpe's ankle still bothered him the following week when Carlisle took on Harvard. But he took the field and had two standout plays: a 55-yard pass completion and a 60-yard run. Neither led to a score, however, and Thorpe's ankle proved to be Carlisle's downfall. They lost their first game of the season 17–0, as Thorpe missed eight field goals.

In the Pennsylvania Mud

Nursing their wounded pride, the Carlisle Indians traveled to Pittsburgh for a game against the University of Western Pennsylvania. The conditions were as bad as they had been against Princeton at New York City's Polo Grounds the previous season. The rain fell, and the teams slogged back and forth on the field. Kicking a successful field goal was hopeless. The game was score- less until late in the fourth quarter when Thorpe slipped and slid in the mud, carrying the ball into the end zone. Final score: Carlisle over Western Pennsylvania, 6–0.

Carlisle then had to play four road games in fifteen days. It was a grueling schedule to end the season. They traveled by long and tiresome train rides. The players passed time on the train with card games and practical jokes. Perhaps they took things a little too lightly. When they played the first of the road games, they lost to the University of Minnesota 11−6.

Carlisle came back and won the last three games. They shut out the University of St. Louis 17−0. They then beat the University of Nebraska 31−6. On a snowy and frozen field, they topped the University of Denver 8−4.

Thorpe especially shone against Nebraska, with a 38-yard run for a touchdown following a fumble recovery. His worst performance occurred against Denver. On one play, he hit the rock-hard ground and fumbled. Thorpe was banged up so badly that he was forced to leave the game. Substitute kicker Pete Hauser converted 2 field goals, accounting for all of Carlisle's points.

Carlisle finished the season with a 10–2–1 record. Jim Thorpe had made a national name for himself. He was honored as a member of the third-team All-America squad.

Chapter

5

The Lure of the Diamond

Ooutside sports, Thorpe was having problems. A new superintendent at Carlisle, Moses Friedman, took over in 1908. Friedman was dismayed by what he saw as a lack of discipline among the students. So he established new rules students had to follow. One stated that every student had to carry a schedule card. The card was marked with classes or other events the student was required to attend. He also abolished popular school-sponsored coed parties.

A Trip Off Campus

Thorpe, at twenty-one years old, was not thrilled with the strict rules. In an act of rebellion, he and another student, Samson Burd, left campus without permission for three days in February 1909. The next month Thorpe left campus again, but for four days. By leaving campus, Thorpe and Burd missed classes.

As punishment, Friedman officially reprimanded the two students. He noted the absences on their school records and sent a letter criticizing Thorpe to the Sac and Fox Indian Agency in Oklahoma. At the same time, Thorpe's grades were declining.

> **"There seemed nothing he could not do."**
>
> **—Pop Warner**

In spite of his disciplinary issues, Thorpe was named captain of the 1909 track team. Based on athletic ability alone, Thorpe deserved the honor. In a meet at Georgetown University in Washington, D.C., he won six gold medals in events that required everything from speed to strength. These were: the 50-yard hurdles, the two 120-yard hurdles, the 50-yard dash, the 100-yard dash, the high jump, and the shot put.

Thorpe then picked up an amazing seven medals in a track meet at Syracuse. He received four gold medals, one silver, and two bronze medals.

Coach Warner later said, "There seemed nothing he could not do, and whenever we needed points to win a meet, I would wait until Jim finished on the track and then throw him in the weight events."[1]

Thorpe stayed on the track squad for the entire season. But as in 1908, Thorpe joined the Carlisle baseball team as soon as track season ended.

Spurring on the Carlisle baseball team was the example set by a Carlisle graduate named Charles Albert "Chief" Bender. ("Chief" was a common nickname for American Indians, but it is considered a racial slur by many.) Carlisle students like Thorpe felt Bender was a fine role model.

Thorpe played the last few games of Carlisle's twenty-seven game baseball season. As soon as the school year was finished, Thorpe looked for opportunities to play baseball for money. Warner reminded Thorpe that he had two more years of eligibility for Carlisle's football team and urged him to stay in school.

But Superintendent Friedman was about to drop baseball from the school's official sports. That troubled players like Thorpe, who saw themselves making money on the diamond when not at school.

Warner had no problem with Friedman's decision. Warner feared that once student athletes realized they could make money playing baseball, they would lose interest in amateur sports like track and football. Friedman was concerned they would drop out of school to play baseball professionally.

Regardless of how much Warner tried convincing him to stay in school, Thorpe was tired of the classes and discipline. Thorpe told Friedman he wanted a summer leave of absence to play baseball. Friedman reluctantly granted Thorpe the leave.

Charles Bender would go on to play for the professional baseball team, the Philadelphia Athletics. Above is his baseball card from 1912.

Charles Albert "Chief" Bender

Charles Albert Bender, a member of the Chippewa tribe, was born on May 5, 1883, at the White Earth Chippewa Indian Reservation in Brainerd, Minnesota. At Carlisle, he played football, basketball, and track as well as baseball. After he graduated from Carlisle in 1902, he attended Dickinson College where he played both baseball and football. While he was playing on his school team, Bender was discovered by a baseball scout for the Philadelphia Athletics (today the Oakland Athletics).

Bender was not the first American Indian to play Major League Baseball, but he was one of the most famous. He played his entire career, from 1903 through 1916, with the Athletics. His best year was 1910 when his pitching record was 23–5, and he finished his career with 212 wins and 127 losses.[2] But he is perhaps best known in baseball history for inventing a pitch called the slider.[3]

After his playing days were over, Bender managed both the Chicago White Sox and New York Giants. He also worked as a scout and coach for the Athletics in the late 1940s and early 1950s. Bender was elected to the National Baseball Hall of Fame in 1953.

Thorpe and the Summer Game

Playing summer baseball was common for student athletes at Carlisle and elsewhere. There were over thirty minor leagues at the time. Thorpe received word that the Rocky Mount Railroaders in North Carolina were looking for players. The Railroaders were part of the seven-team, Class D, Eastern Carolina League. Class D was the lowest ranked of all the minor leagues. (Today there is no Class D. It was discontinued in the early 1960s.)

The Railroaders' season started in May, but Thorpe did not show up until the school year ended in June. While he excelled at track and football, Thorpe had more difficulty with baseball. As a pitcher, he finished the season with a 9–10 record. As a batter, he had a .253 batting average.[4] While his hitting and pitching did not impress fans, his speed did. He amazed opponents by reaching first base on routine ground balls.

As Friedman feared, when baseball season was over, Thorpe did not return to school. He went to Oklahoma where he lived on his sister Mary's farm and did odd chores to earn his keep.

Staying in Touch

Although miles from Carlisle, Thorpe kept in touch with former teammates. He learned that Coach Warner was anxious to have him back on the team. Warner even sent Thorpe a train ticket to Cincinnati,

Ohio, the site of Carlisle's last football game of the 1909 season. Carlisle's opponent was the University of St. Louis, and Cincinnati was a neutral site. Thorpe attended the game and gave the Carlisle players a pep talk. Carlisle won 32−0, but after the cheering ended, Thorpe returned to Oklahoma.

Thorpe and Warner stayed close. They were both avid hunters, so Thorpe invited Warner to Oklahoma to hunt for turkey and deer. Then for Christmas 1909, Thorpe made the long train trip to Carlisle to spend the holiday with his former classmates. After the turkey dinner and exchange of gifts, he went back to Oklahoma again.

When spring came around, Thorpe headed back to North Carolina to play baseball for the Rocky Mount Railroaders. So many Carlisle students left school to play minor league baseball that Carlisle officially dropped the game as a recognized sport.

> In one game, Thorpe broke a scoreless tie in the bottom of the ninth inning.

Thorpe played twenty-nine games for Rocky Mount. He batted only .236, but again impressed crowds with his base running.[5] In one game, Thorpe broke a scoreless tie in the bottom of the ninth inning by scoring from first base on a routine single to left field.

That win was the exception to the rule. The Railroaders lost so many games that fans stopped coming to watch. On July 23, the Railroaders officially disbanded. Thorpe joined another Eastern Carolina League team, the Fayetteville Highlanders, on August 12. In sixteen games for the Highlanders, Thorpe batted .253.[6]

Back Home Again

Once more, Thorpe spent the off-season in Oklahoma. And he played semipro baseball the next spring. This time he played for a hardscrabble team based in Anadarko, Oklahoma, called the Anadarko Champions. The level of play was below that of the Eastern Carolina League. The Champions did not even belong to a formal league, and few statistics were kept. Officially, it was an amateur team, although the players received meager payments.

In one game, Thorpe accomplished an incredible feat. He hit home runs into three different states. The ballpark was located on the spot where Oklahoma, Texas, and Arkansas all meet. His first home run was over the left-field wall and the ball landed in Oklahoma. His second soared over the right-field wall and the ball came down in Arkansas. Then he hit an inside-the-park home run and the ball stayed in Texas.[7]

Thorpe left the Champions in July. One story says he was fired for breaking training rules. Another says that the team could no longer afford to pay him.

A Fateful Meeting

Thorpe had grown tired of drifting between his home and small towns. He realized he had made a mistake by leaving school.[8] One day in the summer of 1911,

55

Thorpe was walking down a street in Anadarko when he met his old friend and mentor Albert Exendine. Exendine told Thorpe that Warner would offer him a chance to try out for the 1912 Summer Olympics. Even without the lure of the upcoming Olympics, Thorpe felt ready to return to Carlisle.

In the two years he had been away from football, more rules had changed. Officials had banned a forward pass of more than twenty yards. Also, a punted ball was a free ball. The punter could run down the field and catch the ball either in the air or on a bounce. Then he could run with it. The passing rule hurt Carlisle, whose quarterbacks routinely threw long passes. However, with speed demons like Thorpe on their team, the punting rule helped them.

There was also a change in scoring. Field goals were worth three points, not four. A touchdown was still five points with a kick for a possible extra point. However, a team now needed four downs, not three, to get a first down.

The Dickinson victory featured an 85-yard touchdown run by Thorpe.

One thing did not change. Carlisle's early games were easy ones. The Indians shut out their first three opponents: Lebanon Valley College 53−0; Muhlenberg College 32−0; and Dickinson College 17−0. The Dickinson victory featured an 85-yard touchdown run by Thorpe. He had three touchdown runs in the next game, a 46−5 win over Mount St. Mary's College. The longest touchdown run in that game was 67 yards.

Word about the talented Thorpe spread across the country. One newspaper article both praised Thorpe and sympathized with the plight of American Indians. The writer's name was listed as Jim Nasium ("gymnasium"). It was actually a pen name for Hugh Miller, a member of Pop Warner's staff.

Carlisle won the season's fifth game 28−5 over Georgetown. Thorpe did not score a touchdown, but he did have a 45-yard run. He also kicked a couple of extra points and was a tough and ready tackler on defense.

Injury

Carlisle shut out its next two opponents. In their 17−0 win against the University of Pittsburgh, Thorpe twice recovered his own punts. One time he grabbed his punt, then danced around a handful of defenders to run 20 yards for a touchdown. Carlisle then defeated Lafayette College 19−0. Thorpe scored a touchdown and kicked a field goal and an extra point. But near the end of the game, he twisted an ankle and was carried off the field.

Warner did not want to lose his star, especially with a game against archrival University of Pennsylvania the next week. Thorpe suited up and practiced before the Penn game, but he was in too much pain to play. Luckily, Pennsylvania's best player, LeRoy Mercer, also sat out the game with an injury. In the end, Carlisle shut out Penn 16−0.

Thorpe was very good at punting the football. He was even able to sometimes recover his own punts.

Playing With Pain

Though not fully healed by the next week, Thorpe played. Carlisle traveled to Massachusetts to take on powerful Harvard. It seemed that everyone took Carlisle seriously except for Harvard coach Percy Haughton. He thought so little of Carlisle that he did not stay to coach the game. Haughton went to Connecticut on a scouting trip, leaving his assistant coaches in charge. He instructed his assistants not to start any regular players. He wanted to save them for a future game against Yale University.

Thorpe was back on the field, but his ankle was encased in adhesive plaster. Because of Thorpe's damaged leg, Warner did not want him carrying the ball. Thorpe mostly played in a defensive role, blocking for other runners. Yet he did boot two field goals, including a 43-yarder. Still, Harvard went into halftime with a 9−6 lead.

Since Carlisle had not yet scored a touchdown, Thorpe was anxious to do his part. Bad ankle or not, he demanded a chance to run with the ball. Warner gave him permission to do so in the second half. The ankle was causing Thorpe much pain, but he made several long runs to set up a touchdown run by running back Alex Arcasa. Shortly after the touchdown, Thorpe attempted another field goal from 37 yards out. He planted the ball through the uprights and the Harvard faithful were stunned to see Carlisle leading the home team 15−9.

Both Harvard and Princeton (pictured above) were tough opponents for the Carlisle team. Princeton actually played the first college football game in history against Rutgers University in New Jersey, on November 6, 1869.

Finally, in the fourth quarter, Harvard brought out their nine starters who had been resting on the bench. The pressure was now on Carlisle's tired defense who had played three quarters of rugged, hard-hitting football. Warner knew his six-point lead was not safe.

Late in the fourth quarter, Carlisle faced a third down on Harvard's 48-yard line. Warner called for a field-goal attempt. Thorpe asked his coach if he was serious. He said the distance was too far for a field goal, and he should punt. Warner insisted, and told Thorpe he could do it.

Thorpe ran up and kicked a low drive. A Harvard defender got his hands on the ball, but not enough to deflect it. The ball kept going. Not only did it split the crossbars, but it sailed 20 yards beyond them before landing. The score was now 18–9, with Carlisle ahead.

That field goal provided the insurance points Carlisle needed. Harvard scored late, and the final outcome was Carlisle 18, Harvard 15. Even with his bad ankle, Thorpe had run 173 yards.

Upset

The players were full of confidence as they took a train to Syracuse, New York, for their next game. A cold and constant rain caused the field in Syracuse's Archbold Stadium to become a mess. Thorpe scored two touchdowns and kicked an extra point. However, he shanked the second extra point attempt on the slippery field. That proved to be the difference as Syracuse upset Carlisle 12−11. Despite his otherwise excellent performance, Thorpe blamed himself for the loss.[9]

Carlisle had an easier time the next week, cruising past Johns Hopkins University 29−6. Thorpe ran for two early touchdowns. Warner then lifted Thorpe and other starters to give second stringers a chance to play. Carlisle played Brown University in the season's last game. On a late November day when rain turned into snow, Thorpe kicked two field goals and an extra point. He also

Thorpe scored two touchdowns and kicked an extra point.

punted once for 83 yards. The final score was Carlisle 12, Brown 6. Except for the loss to Syracuse, Thorpe's team had won every game that season.

On the return trip to Carlisle, Thorpe's teammates voted him team captain for the 1912 season. He learned soon afterward that he was named first team All-America. But before he would play football again, Thorpe was about to debut on a new sports stage in front of the whole world.

Chapter 6

"Let's Show the Army What the Indians Can Do"

Although Thorpe entered Carlisle seven years earlier as a shy, troubled individual, in 1911 he was a big man on campus. In December, he played Santa Claus at the school Christmas party. Dressed in a white beard, red suit, and black boots, the twenty-four-year-old All-American football player handed out presents to his fellow students.

Meeting Iva

The party featured music and dancing. Although Thorpe was at first scared to dance, before long no one could drag him off the dance floor. His favorite partner was an attractive and energetic eighteen-year-old student named Iva Miller, known as Ivy. Like Thorpe, Miller was born in Indian Territory in present-day Oklahoma. Her parents died when she was five. She first attended Chilocco Indian School in Indian Territory. After some time at Chilocco, Miller was sent by her aunt to Carlisle.

It seemed that half the boys at Carlisle had a crush on Miller. Thorpe had chatted with her before, but she was not interested in him. After the acclaim Thorpe achieved during the 1911 football season, Iva Miller took more notice of the tall, athletic, young man. The two soon became a couple.

Thorpe was maturing. Despite his athletic success, Thorpe was humble and had to work at his studies. One of his favorite teachers was Marianne Moore, who later became famous as a talented poet. Moore was also a huge sports fan. Thorpe did favors for her like carrying her umbrella on a cloudy day. Moore said about Thorpe, "Jim is still a bit laborious in the classroom, but he's dependable. Outside the classroom he's modest and casual about everything he has achieved. He is a chivalrous, decent, and cooperative young man."[1]

Back to Track

The 1912 track season began in winter with several indoor meets. At a February meet in Boston, Thorpe set a new school high jump record: 6 feet 1/2 inch. In an early March meet in Pittsburgh, he won four of five events: the running high jump, the 60-yard dash, the 60-yard hurdles, and the shot put. By spring, Carlisle track athletes were thinking about the Summer Olympics.

Thorpe was so highly regarded that he was not required to try out for the majority of Olympic events. The only other athlete so excused was Thorpe's teammate, a Hopi Indian named Louis Tewanima. Thorpe and Tewanima did have to try out for the pentathlon, though. Both passed the pentathlon trial with ease.

June 14, 1912, was one of the most exciting days in Thorpe's life. He, Tewanima, and Warner boarded a passenger ship, the S.S. *Finland*. They sailed past the Statue of Liberty, out of New York Harbor, and out onto the Atlantic Ocean. Fellow passengers included more than 160 United States Olympic team members.

Being aboard the S.S. *Finland* left a huge impression on Thorpe. His daughter Grace once asked him what he liked best about the Olympics. She said he laughed and answered, "'Going over [to Europe] on the boat.'" She added, "You have to remember he had grown up in a small town in Oklahoma. He had never been on a great big ship like that. He liked going around and exploring every part of the ship."[2]

Louis Tewanima

It seems that Louis Tewanima was destined to be a track star. He was born in 1888 on the Hopi Reservation in a place called Second Mesa in present-day Arizona. He worked by tending sheep and planting vegetables, but he spent his spare time running. Sometimes he chased jackrabbits around the reservation. Other times he ran to the town of Winslow, about sixty miles away. He liked to watch trains pass through town.

Shortly after Tewanima arrived at Carlisle, Warner made him a member of the track team. Tewanima repeatedly won ten- and fifteen-mile races against other colleges. In 1908, he represented the United States at the Olympics in London and finished ninth in the marathon. At the 1912 Olympics in Stockholm, Tewanima won a silver medal for the 10,000-meter race. He finished with a time of 32 minutes 6.6 seconds. A native of Finland named Hannes Kolehmainen beat Tewanima by finishing the course in 31 minutes 20.8 seconds. Still, Tewanima's mark stood as an American record for fifty-two years.

After the 1912 Olympics, Tewanima returned home to Arizona. However, he continued running long distance races for years afterward. Tewanima died in January 1969. Today, the Louis Tewanima Foundation sponsors the annual Louis Tewanima Memorial Footrace in his memory.

The U.S. Olympic team members were from all parts of the country and of all nationalities. Thorpe's roommate on board was Abel Kiviat, a Jewish runner from New York City. When they met, Kiviat broke the ice by saying to Thorpe, "We're both tribal people. Mine, being Jewish, that of Abraham."[3]

Practice at Sea

Even at sea, the athletes were expected to practice. Stories about Thorpe's bad attitude toward practice have become legendary. One goes that a newspaper reporter named Francis Albertanti was walking the decks of the S.S. *Finland* and noticed American athletes jumping, running, and practicing in some way. The only exception was Thorpe, who was stretched out on a deck chair.

Albertanti reportedly asked Thorpe, "What are you doing, Jim? Thinking about your uncle, Sitting Bull?" Thorpe responded to the rude question sarcastically, "No, I'm practicing the broad jump. I've just jumped twenty-three feet, eight inches."[4]

According to another tale, the no-nonsense coach of the U.S. track team, Mike Murphy, came across Thorpe rocking in a hammock. Murphy complained to Pop Warner that his protégé Thorpe did nothing but relax while the rest of the track team got into shape.

Warner replied, "Don't worry, Mike. All those two-for-a-nickel events you've got lined up for Thorpe won't bother him. What with football, lacrosse, baseball, and track back at school, how could he be out of shape? This sleeping is the best training ever—for Jim."[5]

On the other hand, perhaps Albertanti and Murphy did not encounter Thorpe at the right time. A sprinter on the track team, Ralph Craig, stated that he spent every day aboard the ship doing calisthenics and running laps with Thorpe right by his side.

The Olympics Get Underway

The official opening ceremonies for the Olympics took place on July 6. Thorpe's first event, the pentathlon, began the next day. Among Thorpe's American competitors was an engineer from Michigan, Avery Brundage.

The first pentathlon test was the running broad jump. Thorpe seemed relaxed as he leaped off the takeoff board and landed 23 feet 2.7 inches away. It was good enough to finish first.

The second event was the javelin throw, a favorite event of Scandinavian athletes. It was not surprising then that Hugo Wieslander from Sweden won it with a toss of more than 162 feet. Thorpe finished in third place. His toss was more than nine feet shorter than Wieslander's.

Thorpe ran like fire in the next event, the 200-meter dash. He finished at 22.9 seconds, a tenth of a second higher than the next two finishers, Americans J. J. Donahue and J. A. Menaul.

The discus throw was fourth. Thorpe managed to hurl the discus 116 feet 8.4 inches, and finish in first

Jim Thorpe throws the discus during the pentathlon event of the 1912 Olympic Games in Stockholm, Sweden.

place. His closest competitor was Brundage, whose throw landed three feet behind Thorpe's.

The Final Pentathlon Event

The pentathlon competitors lined up for the 1,500-meter race. Thorpe might have been a talented sprinter, but 1,500 meters is hardly a quick sprint. Early on in the race, Thorpe was behind most of his competitors. Brundage and Norwegian Ferdinand Bie were vying for the lead position.

During the second lap Thorpe went into overdrive. He passed Brundage, making Bie his prime competitor. Bie was known as a strong finisher, so Thorpe did everything he could to stay with him step for step. Thorpe's endurance wore on Bie. By the last lap, Bie was exhausted. He slowed and fell back in the pack. When the race was over, Bie was in sixth place. Thorpe was the clear winner with a time of 4 minutes 44.8 seconds. His four victories in five events made him the undisputed winner.

Thorpe entered two single events, too. In these, Thorpe proved he was mortal. He finished fourth in the high jump and seventh in the broad jump. But the decathlon was on the horizon, where Thorpe would draw praise from the Swedish king as the greatest athlete in the world.

The Americans did not return home right after the Olympics ended. They journeyed to France where they took part in exhibition track meets. Winners were to be awarded with bottles of champagne. However, the

Thorpe competes in the 110-meter hurdle event during the decathlon at the 1912 Olympics.

athletes were told they were not allowed to accept the champagne. Olympic athletes had to be amateurs. Awards were considered payment. Any athlete who took payment in the form of cash or a material item was officially no longer an amateur.

Heroes

Upon returning to the United States, the entire team was treated as heroes. They were guests of honor in parades in both New York City and Philadelphia. Thorpe said after the New York parade, "I heard people

American athletes are honored with a parade in New York City after returning from the 1912 Olympic Games.

yelling my name, and I couldn't realize how one fellow could have so many friends."[6]

When Thorpe and Tewanima arrived in Carlisle they were honored with banners, crowds, and brass bands. President William Howard Taft sent a telegram of congratulations to Thorpe.

While Thorpe appreciated the fans' support, his daughter Grace said being an idol made him uneasy. She stated, "He was very humble. He never liked talking about himself. It embarrassed him. If he saw a reporter coming to talk to him he'd run the other way."[7]

Thorpe received numerous offers to play professional baseball. However, he did not want to lose his amateur status. He had one more big meet ahead of him. The Amateur Athletic Union (AAU), an organization promoting amateur sports, sponsored the AAU All-Around Championship on September 2. It consisted of ten events. Just days before it began, Thorpe entered a hospital with food poisoning. He was released the day before the meet. Yet he still managed to win most of the events and was named the meet's All-Around Athlete.

Turning Down the Pros

Thorpe had more offers to go professional. But Carlisle football season was coming up, and he had one more year left of football eligibility. Thorpe's son Jack Thorpe later explained, "Coach Warner talked him into staying one more year at Carlisle. All [Jim's] friends were still there. Some of it was the camaraderie with the team and some of it was loyalty to both Warner and his teammates."[8]

Carlisle started out the season with four blowouts: 50−7 over Albright College, 45−0 over Lebanon Valley, 34−0 over Dickinson, and 65−0 over Villanova. However, the next week Jefferson and Washington College held Carlisle to a 0−0 tie. Jefferson and Washington was a small school, but a football dynamo. Thorpe was excellent on defense, making four interceptions. But on offense he missed three field-goal attempts.

After the game, Thorpe and quarterback Gus Welch went to a nearby bar to have some drinks. They then made their way to a hotel restaurant where they continued drinking. When Warner heard that Thorpe was drinking, he tracked him down and yanked him out of the hotel. He forced Thorpe to apologize to his teammates and swear he would never drink alcohol again.

Rematch Against Syracuse

The next week, Carlisle met Syracuse. The Carlisle Indians were anxious for payback against the only team that beat them in 1911. The field was muddy and slippery, and Thorpe had trouble gaining traction. That made him little more than a tackling dummy for the Syracuse defense. Warner pulled Thorpe aside and told him that speed alone would not carry him in the conditions. He instructed Thorpe to emphasize his muscle over his fast feet. In the second half, Thorpe followed his coach's advice and plowed through the Syracuse defensive line, helping Carlisle shut out Syracuse 33−0.

Carlisle clobbered the University of Pittsburgh in the next game 45−8, with Thorpe scoring 34 points. The next week they topped Georgetown University 34−20. The following week, the Indians trekked up to Canada to play the University of Toronto. The game was part of a centennial commemoration of the War of 1812.

In Canadian football, a team can score one point when the ball is kicked into the end zone by an opponent and not returned. The point is called a *rouge*, or a single. In the Carlisle-Toronto match, the first half of the game was played according to American rules.

The 1912 Carlisle football team was ready to take on the Army team. Thorpe is in the back row, at the right.

The second half was played by Canadian rules. Carlisle won by an unusual score of 49−1.

A Fight With the Army

Carlisle remained undefeated by beating Lehigh University 34−14. Their next opponent, the U.S. Military Academy (Army), was known for its massive musclemen. Army's captain Leland Devore weighed 250 pounds, unusual for college football in 1912. Carlisle's biggest man was Thorpe. Just before the game,

Thorpe told his teammates, "All right, boys, let's show the Army what the Indians can do."[9]

Carlisle tromped onto the field in a formation Army had never seen. It was called a wingback, or single wing. The key was keeping halfback Thorpe close to the line. That virtually gave the Indians an eight-man front line. It meant Thorpe would be in position to either run, block, or throw. Warner's simple wing-back formation was the ancestor of more modern football formations.

In the first quarter, Thorpe was tackled hard after a 20-yard run. As he lay on the ground with the wind knocked out of him, the clock ticked away. The referee was about to restart play when Devore told him to wait for Thorpe to get up. Devore did not want to win if he could not beat Carlisle's best. When Thorpe heard that he became even more determined to beat Army's big boys.

Army had its own powerful halfback, a Kansas kid named Dwight Eisenhower. He would grow up to be supreme allied commander in World War II and the thirty-third president of the United States. Both teams scored touchdowns in the first half, but Army missed an extra point, giving Carlisle a halftime lead of 7−6.

The Second Half

The second half was all Carlisle. They scored twenty unanswered points, winning 27−6. As tough a competitor as he was, Devore was gracious in defeat. He said of Thorpe, "That Indian is the greatest player I have ever stacked up against in my five years experience. [He] is super-human, that is all. There is no stopping him!"[10]

Eisenhower said, "Except for [Thorpe], Carlisle would have been an easy team to beat. On the football field, there was no one like him in the world."[11]

Yet as before, Carlisle stumbled following a huge victory. They were thumped in their next game by the University of Pennsylvania 34–26. Thorpe had two touchdowns, including an 80-yard run. He also kicked two extra points. But Warner, frustrated with the loss, criticized Thorpe for being careless and missing an easy interception.

The next to last game of the season was not against a college team. Carlisle's opponent was a team from the Springfield YMCA in Massachusetts. It was thought that the Indians would wipe the floor with the YMCA players, but the boys from Springfield proved a challenge. Carlisle escaped with a 30–24 win. In the audience that day was Charles Clancy, who had been Thorpe's baseball manager a few years earlier in Fayetteville, North Carolina.

Carlisle was victorious its last game of 1912, white-washing Brown University 32–0. Carlisle finished the season with a 12–1–1 record.

Everything seemed rosy for Thorpe. But little did he know that at the Springfield game, Charles Clancy chatted with a newspaper reporter named Roy Johnson. The subject was the time Thorpe played semipro baseball. That conversation would haunt Thorpe for the rest of his life.

7

"I Won Them Fair and Square"

Early in 1913, Jim Thorpe was on top of the world. The people of Carlisle loved him. The nation hailed him as a true hero. His girlfriend adored him, and the couple was discussing marriage.

Thorpe's good feelings did not last long. On January 22, 1913, a headline in a Massachusetts newspaper, the *Worcester Telegram*, read, "Thorpe with Professional Baseball Team Says Clancy."[1]

The name of the article writer was not listed, but it was later discovered to be Roy Johnson.

Following his conversation with Charles Clancy, Johnson did some research and learned Clancy's comments were true. According to the strict rules of the time, that meant that Thorpe was not a pure amateur when he took part in the Olympics.

In the article, Johnson pondered the question of whether or not Thorpe would be allowed to keep his Olympic medals. If the Olympic officials decided that Thorpe broke the rules, then he did not honestly earn his Olympic honors. They would be awarded to the runners-up.

Bigger newspapers elsewhere followed up on the story. At first Pop Warner and American Commissioner to the Olympics John Sullivan told Thorpe to say the story was false—that he never played baseball for money. That would have been an outright lie. It could also be easy to disprove. Financial records and newspaper articles covering Thorpe's playing days were easy to find.

Just a Summer Job?

Thorpe told Warner he did not understand what the big deal was. What did playing semipro baseball a few years earlier have to do with track and field events at the Olympics? To Thorpe and other college athletes, playing summer baseball for little money was no different than taking any summer job, like gardening work. Thorpe said, "I did not know that I was doing wrong because I was doing what I knew several other college men had done."[2]

On January 26, Thorpe met again with Warner and Sullivan. This time they pressured him to sign a confession, admitting that he was paid for playing baseball in 1909 and 1910. Thorpe explained that he chose to play baseball because he loved the game. He also stated that he did not know it was wrong according to amateur sports rules.

Sullivan and Warner also asked Thorpe to swear that neither they nor anyone else at Carlisle were aware that he played baseball for money. That was totally false. But Sullivan and Warner risked their careers if the truth was reported.

A Show of Support

Thorpe's fellow students stood by him. So did the majority of sportswriters. They said Thorpe earned his Olympic medals fair and square. However, the AAU and International Olympic Committee (IOC) disagreed. Thorpe was forced to pack up his medals and ship them to IOC headquarters in Lausanne, Switzerland.

Thorpe was forced to pack up his medals.

Some of Thorpe's fans collected money to purchase duplicates of the Olympian's medals. That way he would have some material evidence of his awards. Thorpe wanted nothing to do with those plans. He asked that any money they collected be given to charity. Because he could no longer compete as an amateur, Thorpe had no choice but to quit Carlisle and openly become a professional. Thorpe was world famous and all sorts of businessmen felt he could make money for them. Warner served as Thorpe's agent, and he would help Thorpe decide the best jobs to take. Warner would also negotiate Thorpe's salary. For his work, Warner would receive a percentage of Thorpe's income.

A Philadelphia boxing promoter named Harry Edwards wanted Thorpe to become a professional prizefighter. Some in the entertainment business thought Thorpe could earn a lot of money traveling the country. He would discuss his life and perform feats of strength. Others believed Thorpe could do well in the new business of motion pictures. A half dozen major-league baseball owners attempted to get Jim to join their teams.

Becoming a Giant

Thorpe discussed his offers with Warner. Since he enjoyed baseball, Thorpe decided to earn a living on the diamond. The Pittsburgh Pirates, Cincinnati Reds, New York Giants, New York Yankees, Chicago White Sox, and St. Louis Browns (today the Baltimore Orioles) all made offers. Because the Giants had won two straight National League pennants, Thorpe opted to play for the Giants as an outfielder.

He was paid a large salary for that time: $4,500 a season for three seasons.[3] That would be equal to about $90,600 per season today.[4]

Unfortunately, Thorpe and Giants manager John McGraw fought often. Playing baseball had always been fun for Thorpe. To McGraw, baseball was work. He expected his players to train constantly and condition themselves. Thorpe reported for spring training in Marlin Springs, Texas, in 1913. He took McGraw's rules lightly, as if he was still playing minor league baseball in the Carolinas.

For example, McGraw's players had a strict curfew, which Thorpe openly defied. It was also reported that Thorpe abused alcohol.[5]

If McGraw barked at Thorpe for not taking rules seriously, Thorpe often played the class clown and responded with a joke. In the middle of one practice, Thorpe and pitcher Jeff Tesreau had an impromptu wrestling match. At one point, Thorpe pinned Tesreau's

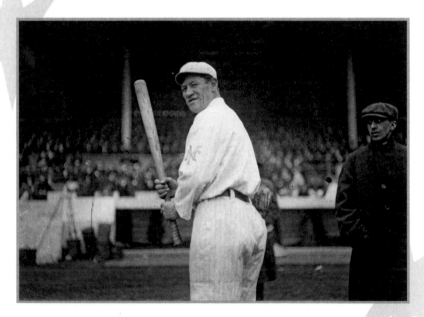

In 1913, Jim Thorpe suited up to join the New York Giants baseball team.

arm behind his back. Tesreau was scheduled to pitch the next day, but he told McGraw he could not because he had a sore arm. McGraw blamed the sore arm on the wrestling match. He threatened to fine Thorpe if he got involved in any more roughhousing.

Thorpe continued to defy his manager. It did not take long for McGraw to send Thorpe down to a Giants' farm team in Milwaukee, where younger players sharpen their skills. That's where Thorpe spent the rest of the 1913 season.

Marriage

Thorpe and Iva Miller married on October 14, 1913, in Carlisle. Thorpe said to his new wife, "Iva, the king of Sweden called me Sir. I guess that means I'm a Lord and if I'm a Lord, then you are my Lady."[6]

Thorpe was often at odds with player-manager John J. McGraw, whose 1912 baseball card is pictured above.

In 1914, Thorpe suited up for another season in the Giants outfield. Again, he and McGraw were at each other's throats. As a result, Thorpe appeared in only thirty games and batted a weak .194 for the season.[7] The only real positive news for Thorpe around that time was the birth of his first child. It was a boy he and Iva named James, Jr.

By 1915, it became clear that Thorpe's professional career was not going to be dominated by baseball. He played in only seventeen games for the Giants that year, batting .231.[8] Rules then did not allow baseball players to become free agents as they can today. A player was on a team until his contract was up, until he retired, or until the team traded him. So Thorpe remained an unhappy Giant.

An Uncommon Discussion

Thorpe was friendly with his teammates, but he never liked discussing the Olympic scandal. On one rare occasion, he confessed his feelings to his Giants roommate, John "Chief" Meyers, also an American Indian. Meyers said that late one night, Thorpe walked

John Meyers was one of Thorpe's best friends on the New York Giants. Above, Meyers plays for the Giants at the Polo Grounds. Meyers's 1911 baseball card is pictured as well.

into their room, crying. According to Meyers, Thorpe said, "'You know, Chief. The King of Sweden gave me those trophies, he gave them to me. But they took them away from me. They're mine, Chief, I won them fair and square.'" Meyers added, "It broke his heart, and he never really recovered."[9]

There was some good news on the horizon for Thorpe in 1915. Football was catching on outside college campuses. That was especially true in Ohio. Jack Cusack was the owner of one professional Ohio team, the Canton Bulldogs. Cusack felt Thorpe could kick-start his team and draw fans.

Tackling Pro Football

In 1915, Thorpe began his professional football career with the Bulldogs. Their opponents were patchwork teams based in Ohio and neighboring states. Thorpe was paid $250 a game.[10] That is about $4,800 a game today.[11]

In those early days of pro football, rules were difficult to enforce. In a game against a team from Massillon, Ohio, the Bulldogs thought they had scored a winning touchdown. Massillon fans immediately stormed the end zone and yanked the ball from the Canton player's grasp. Canton fans reacted angrily and called for the referees to take action. In order to stop a potential riot, the referees declared that the Canton player had fumbled and the game ended in a tie.

Alternating Sports

For the next four years, Thorpe played baseball in the summer and football in the fall. In the middle of the 1917 season, the Giants traded him to the Cincinnati Reds. Thorpe played seventy-seven games for the Reds and hit .247.[12]

Back at home, the Thorpes' three-year-old son, James, Jr., was stricken with a disease called infantile paralysis, or polio. Polio affects the spinal column and brain stem. Today, vaccinations can prevent polio. That was not the case in 1917. James, Jr., died shortly afterward. A teammate named Al Schacht said that after James, Jr.'s death, "Jim was never the same."[13]

It was difficult for the couple to get past the death of their son. Jim and Iva Thorpe became more distant toward each other. But the two decided to stay together as Thorpe's sports career continued. He was traded back to the Giants, then to the Boston Braves (today the Atlanta Braves), early in the 1919 baseball season. Thorpe hit .327 in sixty games in 1919.[14] It was his best year as a major league baseball player. It was also his last year. Thorpe then put all his energy into pro football.

Thorpe and the Birth of the NFL

During the off-season in 1920, Thorpe attended a meeting that forever changed professional football. It took place in, of all places, a car dealership in Canton. The dealership owner, Ralph Hay, was also the

Bulldogs' manager. The representatives of ten other football teams were there. They sat on fenders and the backs of cars and discussed forming a pro football league.

One participant, George Halas, was the player-coach of an Illinois team called the Decatur Staleys. The next year, the Staleys moved to Chicago and became the Chicago Bears. Halas discussed the result of the meeting by briefly saying, "In two hours we created the American Professional Football Association."[15] Only two years later, the American Professional Football Association changed its name to the National Football League (NFL).

At the 1920 meeting, Thorpe was elected league president. That was mainly because his fame would bring publicity to the new league. Thorpe was in fact a poor businessman and remained president for just a year. He did not care. He mainly wanted to play.

Although professional football was organized, it had a small following compared to college football and professional baseball. Professional football players were poorly paid. The millions of dollars today's pro football players get would have been a wild fantasy to Thorpe and his fellow gridiron masters.

Now in his early thirties, Thorpe was past his prime for a punishing contact sport like football. Yet he played with Canton in 1920, then with a team in Cleveland in 1921.

Despite their marriage problems, the Thorpes had three more children. In 1921 their daughter Grace was born. They also had two more daughters, Gail and Charlotte.

Introducing the Oorang Indians

For the 1922 season, Thorpe founded a team consisting entirely of American Indians. It was based in LaRue, Ohio, about sixty miles north of Columbus in the central part of the state. Thorpe named the team after its sponsor, Oorang Kennels in LaRue. In exchange, Oorang Kennels supplied Thorpe with Airedale hunting dogs.

For two years, Thorpe's Oorang Indians were the biggest draw in the National Football League. Most of Thorpe's teammates were fellow graduates of Carlisle. The main draw was the novelty of an all-American Indian team. During halftime, Thorpe and the rest of the Oorang Indians entertained the crowds. They played stereotypical roles of American Indians, throwing tomahawks or knives. Consisting of players in their mid-thirties, the Oorang Indians did not do well. Their record was 3–6 in 1922 and 1–10 in 1923. The Indians folded after the 1923 season, but Thorpe was still in demand. He was signed to play the 1924 season with an Illinois team, the Rock Island Independents.

Divorce and New Marriage

Off the football field, Thorpe's life was not happy. He and Iva finally divorced in 1924. Not long afterward, Thorpe began dating a much younger woman named

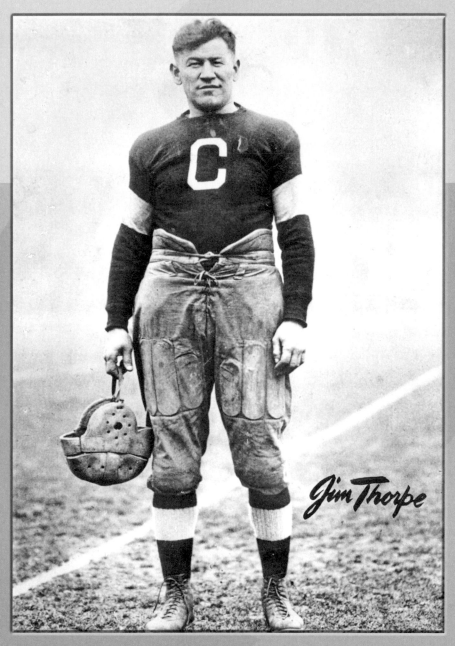

Jim Thorpe

Not only did Thorpe play for teams in the American Professional Football Association (APFA) and the National Football League, he was also president of the APFA during its first year. Above, Thorpe poses in his Canton Bulldogs uniform.

It was discovered in 2005 that not only did Thorpe play baseball and football, he also played basketball professionally—at least for one game.

Thorpe's Other Sport

For a long time, it was believed the only professional team sports Thorpe played after college were baseball and football. Then in 2005, a bombshell discovery was made.

That year, a brother and sister named Anthony and Lee Barone bought an antique book at an auction in Pennsylvania. Buried amid the pages was a ticket stub from a 1927 basketball game. The stub read, "Jim Thorpe and his World Famous Indians" to play against "Clothes Shop."[16] None of Thorpe's descendents was aware that he had played basketball as either a semiprofessional or a full professional.[17]

An investigation showed that the ticket stub is genuine. Researchers from the television program *History Detectives* uncovered a clipping from an Ohio newspaper, *The Marion Star*. It was dated December 24, 1927. The clipping reads: "Jim Thorpe's world famous Indians to meet. Team led by famous Indian will furnish attraction for local basketball fans."[18]

It was proof that Thorpe earned money playing basketball, too. It seems that he played every major team sport except ice hockey.

Freeda Kirkpatrick. On October 23, 1925, they were married.

Thorpe began the 1925 season playing for the New York Giants football team. He was thirty-eight, old for a football player. A few weeks into the season, the Giants released Thorpe for being out of shape. The Rock Island Independents must have disagreed with the Giants because they hired him back.

Thorpe began a new family with Freeda. They had four sons over the next few years—Carl Phillip, William, Richard, and John, known by the nickname Jack—as Thorpe bounded from one football team to another. He played the 1926 season again with Canton. Some accounts say he may have also played for teams in St. Petersburg, Florida; Portsmouth, Ohio; and Hammond, Indiana.[19] Thorpe finished his career in 1928 with the Chicago Cardinals (today the Arizona Cardinals). At the age of forty-one, Thorpe hung up his football helmet for the last time.

Of all the sports Thorpe played, which did he like the most? Thorpe's daughter Grace once asked her father that question. She later remembered: "He said, 'I like hunting and fishing the best.' I laughed and he said, 'Oh, you mean what competitive sport. I like track and field.' It was something he could do by himself. He liked being able to make his own decisions."[20]

Thorpe had been paid what was decent money for the time. However, he had a large family to support. All he had known for his adult life was sports. How would he earn money now? What would he do with the rest of his life?

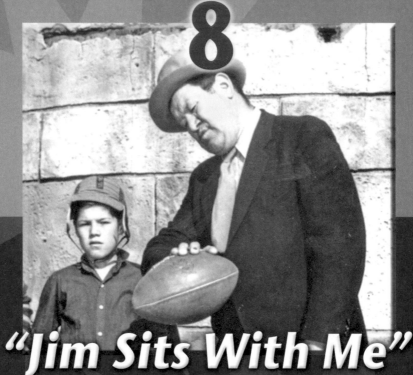

"Jim Sits With Me"

[I]f Thorpe could no longer make a lot of money participating in sports, perhaps he could cash in on his past glories. He sold the rights to his biography to MGM movie studios in Los Angeles. He then moved to California to be on hand for the filming of the movie, *Red Son of Carlisle*. Yet not all planned movies are made. That was the case with *Red Son of Carlisle*.

With his movie option gone, Thorpe tried announcing live sports. He signed up as master of ceremonies for the 1930 version of a cross-country road race called the International Transcontinental Footrace. Reporters called the race "The Great

Bunion Derby." It was to be run in stretches over the course of a few months.

The Great Bunion Derby, which had been held in 1928 and 1929, was the idea of sports promoter Charlie C. Pyle. By the time Thorpe became involved with the race, the Great Depression had hit the United States. Millions of Americans were out of work. Many businesses failed, including the Great Bunion Derby. Thorpe had to sue to get the fifty dollars Charlie Pyle owed him.

Strapped for money, Thorpe took a job in February 1930 as a painter for an oil company. Thorpe, who twenty years earlier received honors from Swedish royalty, was now spending his days painting oil trucks and gas stations.

Actor

By October, Thorpe was no longer needed as a painter. He decided to take advantage of his fame. Although MGM did not make *Red Son of Carlisle*, they hired Thorpe to play an American Indian chief in a small role in a western. He was then given additional small roles in sports movies. But this was an unreliable way to support a family. Thorpe needed steady work, and he resorted to any job he could get. This included manual labor on the site of a new hospital.

Despite the tough times, the early 1930s were an exciting time in Los Angeles. The city was going to host the 1932 Summer Olympics. The world was coming to California and big plans were in the works.

American athlete Jim Thorpe visits his daughter, Grace, in February 1931 at the Haskell Institute, the American Indian school that he once attended in Lawrence, Kansas.

Thorpe may have been stripped of his medals, but he was still a hero to many. So it seemed likely that the star of the 1912 Olympics would be an honored guest at the 1932 games. Yet no Olympic official invited him to be a guest of honor. Even sadder, Thorpe could not afford to buy an admission ticket for himself. It appeared that the former greatest athlete in the world would not even be able to attend the Olympics as a spectator.

A Huge Response

When word got out that Thorpe could not afford to attend the Summer Olympics, Americans across the country wrote protest letters to AAU headquarters. Newspaper editorial writers spoke out in shock and anger.

In response, thousands of Americans volunteered to give Thorpe their tickets. One was Charles Curtis, vice president of the United States. Like Thorpe, Curtis was an American Indian. Curtis spent part of his youth growing up on a reservation in Kansas. The vice president said plainly, "Jim sits with me."[1] When Thorpe took his seat in the presidential box, the crowd of one hundred five thousand gave him a standing ovation.

Once the Olympics were over, Thorpe again became just another American trying to earn a living in the Great Depression. He continued to try to capitalize on his name. A book ghostwritten by an author named T. F. Collison and titled *Jim Thorpe's History of the Olympics* sold poorly.

1932 Summer Olympics

To prepare for the competitions, the city of Los Angeles expanded the city's nine-year-old Coliseum Olympic Stadium in Exposition Park. About twenty-five thousand additional seats were built, bringing the capacity to one hundred five thousand people. That was more than the population of many cities.

It was the first Summer Olympics to use automatic timing for track events and a photo-finish camera for very close races. It was also the first Olympics to use a separate Olympic Village to house athletes. However, only the male athletes stayed in the Olympic Village. Female athletes stayed in a Los Angeles hotel.

A total of eighteen world records were either broken or tied in Los Angeles.[2] One of the biggest stars was American track performer Mildred "Babe" Didrikson. She won two gold medals in the javelin toss and 80-meter hurdles and a silver medal in the high jump. After the Olympics, she played professional golf and is today regarded as one of the best golfers—male or female—in the sport's history.

Thorpe also spoke to school groups, but much of the time he was too kindhearted to take any payment. He also played small roles in westerns with titles such as *Prairie Schooners* and *Wild Horse Mesa*.

Trying to End the BIA

Late in 1937, Thorpe became involved in a political issue. He returned to Oklahoma to try to convince his fellow Sac and Fox to support a bill to abolish the U.S. Bureau of Indian Affairs (BIA). The BIA has many duties. One is managing the American Indian reservations. Thorpe and other American Indians felt the BIA was not fair to them. Some thought the BIA was demeaning to American Indians. Thorpe said, "The Indian should be permitted to shed his inferiority complex and live like a normal American citizen."[3] But the bill was defeated in the U.S. House of Representatives by a vote of 202 to 120.[4]

Thorpe continued to travel to find work. His daughter Grace said that working odd jobs did not bother him. She admitted that in some ways he preferred them. She said, "Dad took life the way it was. He didn't like nine-to-five jobs."[5]

However, Grace also admitted that her father never totally got over his alcohol problem. She said that on one hand, "We never had alcohol around the house. Not even beer."[6] On the other hand, Grace said he would drink outside of home. She noted, "One reason why he probably couldn't hold a nine to five job was his drinking problem. You can't have someone working for

Jim Thorpe gives some passing tips to his sons, Phil, age thirteen (left), and Bill, age eleven, on a movie set in Los Angeles on April 4, 1940. The boys are acting in a movie based on the life of Knute Rockne.

you who takes off every few weeks to go on a bender [a period of heavy drinking].[7]

Divorce, Again

At times, Thorpe toured the country giving lectures about football, his career, or American Indian culture. At one point, he worked as a security guard at an automobile assembly plant near Detroit. As the 1930s rolled into the 1940s, Thorpe's situation did not improve. In 1941, Freeda sued him for divorce.

Thorpe's daughter Grace guessed that one reason for the divorce was her father being away from home so much. She explained that it was natural for American Indian men to roam. That trait was traced back to an earlier time when American Indian men would go away for days to hunt buffalo. Grace said that lifestyle is hard to understand for those who are not American Indians.[8]

Thorpe's son Jack added that it was not always his father's choice to travel. He stated that the nature of Thorpe's work giving lectures forced him away from home a lot. Jack said, "Athletes back then didn't make the money that they do today. He had to do something to make a living once he retired from sports, and he didn't have a trade. So he went on the road to do lectures. Being on the road so much, your family life suffers."[9]

When Jim was home, he made sure to spend time with his children and to teach them what he knew. When things were difficult, he would encourage them— even if it meant being tough. Jack recalled:

We'd go hunting and fishing and camping. He [Jim Thorpe] tried to teach us to kick and pass a football and hit a baseball. He tried to teach us to run and one time I told him I can't do it. He grabbed me up and said, "Don't ever say 'can't' around me. There's no such thing as 'can't.'"[10]

After the United States entered World War II in December 1941, Thorpe tried to join the military. Yet no branch of the service would take a fifty-four-year-old man. So in March 1942, he embarked on yet another lecture tour.

Less than a year later, Thorpe suffered a heart attack. That put Thorpe's name in the news again. It also got Americans thinking about his treatment by the IOC and AAU thirty years earlier.

One Dream

Around that time, Thorpe said, "In the twilight of my life, the one thing I dream of constantly is that the American people will try to get back for me the Olympic trophies I won in 1912. I'd be the happiest man in the world if I could just get my medals back."[11]

The Oklahoma House of Representatives introduced an official resolution. It called for the AAU to return Thorpe's medals to him and add his original marks to the Olympic records. Sportswriters across the country pleaded with the AAU to do what they considered the right thing. According to Grace Thorpe, her father said, "'I never once wrote a letter requesting that

I get the medals back. But others did it for me.'"[12] Grace continued, "He was a humble man. He just was never interested in promoting himself."[13] Efforts to get Thorpe's medals back were ignored by the AAU and the Olympic Committee.

However, there were some high points in Thorpe's life in 1945. On June 2, he married a Louisville woman named Patricia "Patsy" Gladys Askew. Patsy was a successful businesswoman. She felt her husband was being taken advantage of by some groups that hired him to speak. She urged him to charge a fair rate, and he took her advice. Groups he spoke to would also pay his expenses, such as travel, lodging, and meals.

Doing His Part

He was also granted his wish of serving his country. Although the war was winding down, the U.S. Merchant Marines accepted Thorpe for duty. (Merchant marines transport goods across the world. In times of war they also transport troops and supplies for the military.) Thorpe worked as a carpenter on his assigned ship, the U.S.S. *Southwest Victory*. The ship sailed to India to bring ammunition to American and British soldiers. Thorpe also served a dual purpose by visiting wounded soldiers at the base hospital. They were delighted to meet a sports legend.

Thorpe returned home on September 7, 1945, and went back on the lecture circuit. Patsy served as his business manager, ensuring that he was fairly paid. Local dignitaries, such as city mayors, often greeted him. Again, sports writers and fans embarked on campaigns to put Thorpe's records back in the official Olympic books and his medals back in his possession. Time and time again, those requests were ignored.

In 1948, Thorpe was hired to work for the Chicago Department of Recreation. Thorpe spent his days teaching kids from poor neighborhoods the basics of track and field.

Though he was now over sixty, Thorpe showed the public he was no doddering old man. In an old timers' baseball game at Chicago's Wrigley Field, Thorpe belted a 384-foot home run off Baseball Hall of Famer Red Faber. At halftime of a football game between the San Francisco 49ers and the Baltimore Colts (today the Indianapolis Colts) Thorpe was the star of a field-goal kicking exhibition.

In September 1948, he used his football skills to help train the Israel National Soccer Team for a match against the U.S. Olympic Soccer Team. The setting was New York's Polo Grounds, his home stadium when he played baseball for the New York Giants many years earlier. During halftime, Thorpe gave another kicking exhibition. The sixty-one-year-old booted three success-ful 50-yard field goals out of ten attempts.

Finally, the Movie

Then in 1949, Thorpe learned that a movie biography would finally be made. Since he sold the rights to his life story years earlier, Thorpe made no money for the use of his name. However, he did take a paying job as a

Burt Lancaster (center) played Thorpe in Jim Thorpe—All American.

technical adviser for the movie. The original title, *Red Son of Carlisle*, was scrapped. Instead, the movie was titled *Jim Thorpe—All-American*. Burt Lancaster, one of Hollywood's most talented actors, played Thorpe. Filming took place through much of 1949 and 1950.

The year 1950 was a milestone. Journalists and historians reflected on the first half of the twentieth century. The Associated Press polled sports media across the United States. They were asked to rank the twentieth century's best football players. Thorpe was voted number one.

Better Than the Babe

An even bigger honor went to Thorpe shortly afterward. In another survey, 393 sports writers and broadcasters were asked to name the greatest athlete of any kind in the first half of the twentieth century. Thorpe finished first, with 875 points. In second place was baseball great Babe Ruth with 539 points.[14]

Thorpe was in more demand than ever as a public speaker. At Carlisle, a stone tablet monument was dedicated in Thorpe's honor. In a brief speech, Thorpe broke from personal tradition and publicly criticized the decision that cost him his Olympic medals. In Philadelphia, he was awarded the key to the city. In Canton, Ohio, he received a cash prize of one thousand dollars and a wristwatch. An inscription on the wristwatch read, "Jim Thorpe, Canton Bulldogs. From your many friends in Canton, the cradle of professional football."[15]

The speaker at the Canton ceremony was Branch Rickey. When Rickey was the general manager of the Brooklyn Dodgers, he took a courageous step by signing African American baseball player Jackie Robinson in 1945. In doing so, he broke a long-standing color barrier. At the Canton ceremony, Rickey remarked that Thorpe deserved his medals back. In attendance were four U.S. congressmen who served on the Indian Affairs Subcommittee.

The congressmen raised the issue to the entire subcommittee. Shortly afterward, it unanimously approved to have Thorpe's medals restored. Yet once again, the AAU and Olympic officials ignored their request.

The movie *Jim Thorpe—All-American* was released in 1951 and was a huge hit. Thorpe was living with his daughter Grace in Pearl River, New York, at the time. Pearl River is not far from New York City. Grace Thorpe recalled an amusing incident that took place after the movie came out:

> *Dad was doing business in the city [New York] at the time. One time he took a bus into the city and wouldn't you know it—the bus stop was right underneath a movie theater marquee. There he was—holding a leather suitcase and standing under the marquee that read, "Jim Thorpe—All American."[16]*

In November 1951, Thorpe, a cigarette smoker, noticed a sore on his lower lip.[17] After the sore did not heal over several days, Thorpe checked himself in to a hospital. Doctors recognized the sore as cancerous. While Thorpe had some money saved up, he did not have enough to pay for cancer surgery. His fans came through. People everywhere sent nickels, dimes, and dollars to save Thorpe's life. The cancer was caught in time, and Thorpe survived it.

But in the fall of 1952, he suffered a second heart attack. Then he suffered a third on March 28, 1953. This time it was more serious. Thorpe died that same day. There were tributes from all over. But would Thorpe, even in death, ever get the ultimate tribute— the return of his medals and his good name?

Chapter 9

Officially the Greatest

A t the time of Thorpe's death, his former football opponent from Army, Dwight Eisenhower, was president of the United States. When he heard the sad news, Eisenhower sent a personal condolence telegram to Patsy Thorpe.

The California Senate was in session when word of Thorpe's death reached them. In tribute, it immediately adjourned. Several states pronounced formal resolutions honoring the much-loved athlete.

No official plans had been made regarding Thorpe's burial site. Some family members wanted his body brought back to Oklahoma. Many wished

Because of football pioneers like Jim Thorpe, today the sport is one of the two most popular in the United States. Many kids play Pop Warner Football, an organization started by Thorpe's former coach.

From Mauch Chunk to Jim Thorpe

Patsy Thorpe had heard that a small town near the Pocono Mountains in eastern Pennsylvania named Mauch Chunk had an enterprising civic program. It was called the "nickel-a-week-plan." Each citizen of Mauch Chunk contributed a nickel a week to a fund used to attract industry. Patsy liked the idea of every citizen doing his or her part to make their community better.

She visited Mauch Chunk and suggested to local officials that the town might be a good place for her husband's burial site and memorial. She also had one more suggestion—that the town's name be changed from Mauch Chunk to Jim Thorpe.

At first, officials thought that was absurd. Then they spoke to the citizens of Mauch Chunk and discovered that many loved the idea. So the name Mauch Chunk was officially changed to Jim Thorpe. An official memorial to Thorpe was dedicated there on May 30, 1957. About fifteen thousand people attended the event. Thorpe's old friend and teammate, Al Schacht, served as the master of ceremonies.

Olympian Jim Thorpe's burial crypt in Jim Thorpe, Pennsylvania, is inscribed with King Gustav of Stockholm Sweden's statement, "Sir, you are the greatest athlete in the world."

that Thorpe's resting place would be part of a memorial between a baseball diamond and football field there. However, the memorial they had in mind would have cost several thousand dollars. The Thorpe family did not have that much money. The governor of Oklahoma first seemed interested in helping raise funds for the memorial but changed his mind.

Halls of Fame

In 1963, Thorpe was enshrined in the first class in the Professional Football Hall of Fame in Canton, Ohio.

When visitors enter the hall of fame today, one of the first exhibits they see is a seven-foot-high statue of Thorpe in action.

Thorpe has also been inducted into several other halls of fame. These include the College Football Hall of Fame in South Bend, Indiana; the National Track and Field Hall of Fame in New York City; and the National Indian Hall of Fame in Anadarko, Oklahoma. In 1967, the home where he and Iva lived for a while in Yale, Oklahoma, was opened to the public as a museum.

Restoring the Records

It took until October 13, 1982, for Thorpe to receive the honor that eluded him in his lifetime. The International Olympic Committee finally agreed to restore to Thorpe his 1912 Olympics records. In January 1983, his medals were officially presented to Thorpe's descendents.

On April 17, 1999, in an official resolution by the U.S. House of Representatives, Jim Thorpe was declared the "Greatest Athlete of the Twentieth Century." Long after his death, Thorpe still had star power. At an auction in October 2003, a football jersey he once wore was sold. The winner paid $210,000 dollars for it.[1] Even though it was seventy-five years after Jim Thorpe played his last college football game, he still had diehard fans.

Jim Thorpe's Team Sports Statistics

College Football

Year	Rushing			Passing		Scoring	
	Carries	Yards	Average	Attempts	Completions	Touchdowns	Field Goals
1907	16	67	4.2	0	0	6	0
1908	113	781	6.9	13	8	4	6
1911	113	899	8.0	4	1	14	7
1912	191	1869	9.8	18	8	29	4

Major League Baseball

Team	Year	Games	Hits	Doubles	Triples	Home Runs	Average
New York Giants	1913	19	5	0	0	1	.143
New York Giants	1914	30	6	1	0	0	.194
New York Giants	1915	17	12	3	1	0	.231
Cincinnati Reds	1917	77	62	2	8	4	.247
New York Giants	1917	26	11	3	2	0	.193
New York Giants	1918	58	28	4	4	1	.248
New York Giants	1919	2	1	0	0	0	.333
Boston Braves	1919	60	51	7	3	1	.327
	CAREER	289	176	20	18	7	.252

CHRONOLOGY

1887—James Francis Thorpe, also known as Jacobus Franciscus Thorpe, born May 22 in Indian Territory, near present-day Prague, Oklahoma.

ca. 1893—Begins school at Sac and Fox Indian Agency School.

late 1896 or early 1897—Twin brother Charles dies.

1898—Attends school at Haskell Institute in Lawrence, Kansas.

1901—Returns home to work on family farm; runs away to Texas to work on a ranch.

1902—Attends Garden Grove School near family home.

1904—June 1: Begins school at Carlisle Indian Industrial School (CIIS) in Carlisle, Pennsylvania.

1907—Asked to join Carlisle's track team by Coach Pop Warner.

1907–1908, 1911–1912—Plays on Carlisle's track squad and football team.

1909—Summer: Plays pro baseball for minor league Class D Rocky Mount Railroaders.

1909—Fall: Drops out of Carlisle and moves back to Oklahoma.

1910—Summer: Plays pro baseball for minor league Class D Rocky Mount Railroaders and Fayetteville Highlanders.

1911—Summer: Plays baseball for semipro team Anadarko Champions.

1911—**Fall:** Reenrolls at Carlisle Indian Industrial School.

1912—**July:** Wins pentathlon and decathlon at Summer Olympics in Stockholm, Sweden.

September 2: Shines at post-Olympic event, the AAU All-Around Championship.

1913—**January 22:** Thorpe's years as (minor league) professional baseball player first made public. **January 26:** In writing, Thorpe confesses playing professional baseball; forced to return Olympic medals.

1913–1915, 1917–1919—Plays Major League Baseball at various times with New York Giants, Cincinnati Reds, and Boston Braves.

1913—**October 14:** Marries Iva Miller.

1914—Son James, Jr., is born.

1915—Plays early form of professional football for Canton Bulldogs.

1917—Son James, Jr., dies of infantile paralysis (polio).

1920—Named president of newly formed American Professional Football Association (APFA), forerunner of National Football League (NFL); holds position for one year.

1920–1928—Plays professional football at various times for many APFA/NFL teams.

1924—Divorces Iva Thorpe.

1925—**October 23:** Marries Freeda Kirkpatrick.

1930—Signed to be master of ceremonies for failed cross-country road race, the Great Bunion Derby.

1930–1940s—Works odd jobs; takes small roles in Hollywood western movies; travels the country doing lectures.

1932—Attends Summer Olympics in Los Angeles as guest of Charles Curtis, vice president of the United States.

1937—Publicly supports U.S. House of Representatives bill to abolish U.S. Bureau of Indian Affairs

1941—Divorces Freeda Thorpe.

1945—**June 2:** Marries Patricia "Patsy" Gladys Askew.

1945—Joins U.S. Merchant Marines briefly before end of World War II.

1948—Works with young people at Chicago Department of Recreation; hits 384-foot home run in Old Timers' Game at Wrigley Field in Chicago; coaches Israeli National Soccer team; kicks three, 50-yard field goals in exhibition.

1950—Selected as greatest football player of first half of the twentieth century; selected as greatest name in sports for first half of the twentieth century.

1951—Biographical movie, *Jim Thorpe—All American*, released.

1953—**March 28:** Dies of heart attack.

1957—**May 30:** Official Jim Thorpe memorial dedicated in town of Mauch Chunk, Pennsylvania, which changes its name to Jim Thorpe, Pennsylvania.

1963—Enshrined in inaugural class of Professional Football Hall of Fame in Canton, Ohio.

1982—**October 13:** International Olympic Committee agrees to posthumously restore Olympic medals to Thorpe.

1999—**April 17:** U.S. House of Representatives declares Jim Thorpe greatest athlete of the twentieth century.

CHAPTER NOTES

CHAPTER 1
Fit for a King

1. Joseph Bruchac, *Jim Thorpe: Original All-American* (New York: Dial Books, 2006), p. 38.
2. *Jim Thorpe: World's Greatest Athlete*, Official Site of Jim Thorpe, n.d., <http://www.cmgworldwide.com/sports/thorpe/quotes.htm> (October 29, 2006).
3. Ibid.

CHAPTER 2
At Home on the Prairie

1. The Associated Press and Grolier, *Pursuit of Excellence: The Olympic Story* (Danbury, Conn.: Grolier Enterprises, Inc., 1979), p. 68.
2. Gene Schoor, *The Jim Thorpe Story: America's Greatest Athlete*(New York: Pocket Books, 1972), p. 22.
3. Ibid., p. 23.
4. Ron Flatter, "Thorpe preceded Deion, Bo," *ESPN.com*, © 2007 <http://espn.go.com/sportscentury/features/00016499.html (October 29, 2006).
5. Robert W. Wheeler, *Jim Thorpe: World's Greatest Athlete* (Norman, Okla.: University of Oklahoma Press, 1975), p. 17.
6. Schoor, p. 27.

CHAPTER 3
To the Gridiron

1. Personal interview with Grace Thorpe, May 14, 2007.
2. Personal interview with Jack Thorpe, March 17, 2008.

3. Bill Crawford, *All American: The Rise and Fall of Jim Thorpe* (Hoboken, N.J.: John Wiley & Sons, Inc., 2005), p. 56.

4. Robert W. Wheeler, *Jim Thorpe: World's Greatest Athlete* (Norman, Okla.: University of Oklahoma Press, 1975), p. 50.

5. Personal interview with Kent Stephens, Museum Historianand Curator, College Football Hall of Fame, March 14,2008, citing the 2007 edition of the *NCAA Division IFootball Records Book*, p. 127.

6. John S. Watterson, "Inventing Modern Football," *AmericanHeritage*, September/October 1988, p. 106.

7. Ibid., p. 113.

8. Crawford, p. 77.

9. Gene Schoor, *The Jim Thorpe Story: America's Greatest Athlete* (New York: Pocket Books, 1972), p. 41.

CHAPTER 4
Shining at Carlisle

1. Bill Crawford, *All American: The Rise and Fall of Jim Thorpe* (Hoboken, N.J.: John Wiley & Sons, Inc., 2005), p. 78.

2. Ibid., p. 77.

3. Joseph Bruchac, *Jim Thorpe: Original All-American* (New York: Dial Books, 2006), p. 105.

4. Ibid., p. 106.

5. Ibid.

6. Paul Healey, *Project Ballpark*, © 2002–2005, <http://www.projectballpark.org/history/nl/polo2.html> (December 27, 2006).

7. Philip J. Lowry, *Green Cathedrals* (Reading, Mass.: Addison-Wesley Publishing Co., Inc., 1992), p. 196.

8. Ibid., p. 197.

9. Ibid., p. 196.

10. Ibid.

11. Bruchac, p. 108.

12. Robert W. Wheeler, *Jim Thorpe: World's Greatest Athlete* (Norman, Okla.: University of Oklahoma Press, 1975), p. 60.
13. Personal interview with Jack Thorpe, March 17, 2008.
14. Ibid.
15. Personal interview with Kent Stephens, Museum Historian and Curator, College Football Hall of Fame, March 14, 2008.
16. Bruchac, pp. 122–23.
17. Ibid., p. 67.
18. Crawford, p. 112.
19. Bruchac, p. 143.

CHAPTER 5
The Lure of the Diamond

1. Bill Crawford, *All American: The Rise and Fall of Jim Thorpe* (Hoboken, N.J.: John Wiley & Sons, Inc., 2005), p. 115.
2. *National Baseball Hall of Fame & Museum*, © 2008, <http://www.baseballhalloffame.org/hofers/detail.jsp?playerId=110850> (March 15, 2008).
3. *National Baseball Hall of Fame & Museum* © 2008, <http://www.baseballhalloffame.org/hofers_and_honorees/hofer_bios/Bender_Chief.htm> (January 2, 2007).
4. Crawford, p. 125.
5. Joseph Bruchac, *Jim Thorpe: Original All-American* (New York: Dial Books, 2006), p. 166.
6. Ibid., p. 167.
7. *Jim Thorpe: World's Greatest Athlete*, Official Site of Jim Thorpe, n.d., <http://www.cmgworldwide.com/sports/thorpe/fastfacts.htm> (October 29, 2006).
8. Gene Schoor, *The Jim Thorpe Story: America's Greatest Athlete* (New York: Pocket Books, 1972), p. 61.
9. Robert W. Wheeler, *Jim Thorpe: World's Greatest Athlete* (Norman, Okla.: University of Oklahoma Press, 1975), pp. 94–95.

CHAPTER 6
"Let's Show the Army What the Indians Can Do"

1. Joseph Bruchac, *Jim Thorpe: Original All-American* (New York: Dial Books, 2006), p. 206.
2. Personal interview with Grace Thorpe, May 14, 2007.
3. Bruchac, p. 208.
4. Richard Schaap, *An Illustrated History of the Olympics*, (New York: Alfred A. Knopf, 1963), p. 125.
5. Ibid., p. 126.
6. Greg Botelho, "Roller-coaster life of Indian icon, sports' first star," *CNN*, July 14, 2004, <http://www.cnn.com/2004/WORLD/europe/07/09/jim.thorpe/> (May 9, 2007).
7. Personal interview with Grace Thorpe, May 14, 2007.
8. Personal interview with Jack Thorpe, March 17, 2008.
9. Gene Schoor, *The Jim Thorpe Story: America's Greatest Athlete* (New York: Pocket Books, 1972), p. 96.
10. Robert W. Wheeler, *Jim Thorpe: World's Greatest Athlete* (Norman, Okla.: University of Oklahoma Press, 1975), p. 132.
11. Larry Schwartz, "No limits," *ESPN.com*, © 2007 <http://espn.go.com/sportscentury/features/00194728.html> (May 9, 2007).

CHAPTER 7
"I Won Them Fair and Square"

1. Joseph Bruchac, *Jim Thorpe: Original All-American* (New York: Dial Books, 2006), p. 247.
2. Jim Thorpe, *Native Americans* Web site, 2007, <http://www.nativeamericans.com/JimThorpe.htm> (August 3, 2006).
3. Gene Schoor, *The Jim Thorpe Story: America's Greatest Athlete* (New York: Pocket Books, 1972), p. 117
4. S. Morgan Friedman, *The Inflation Calculator*, n.d., <www.westegg.com/inflation> (May 9, 2007).

5. Larry Schwartz, "No limits," *ESPN.com*, © 2007, <http://espn.go.com/sportscentury/features/00194728.html> (May 9, 2007).

6. Bruchac, p. 261.

7. *Baseball-Reference.com*, June 26, 2008, <http://www.baseball-reference.com/t/thorpji01.shtml> (January 17, 2007).

8. Ibid.

9. Lawrence S. Ritter. *The Glory of Their Times: The Story of the Early Days of Baseball Told by the Men Who Played It* (New York: Macmillan, 1966), p. 175.

10. Bill Crawford, *All American: The Rise and Fall of Jim Thorpe* (Hoboken, N.J.: John Wiley & Sons, Inc., 2005), p. 226.

11. S. Morgan Friedman, *The Inflation Calculator.*

12. *Baseball-Reference.com*.

13. Robert W. Wheeler, *Jim Thorpe: World's Greatest Athlete* (Norman, Okla.: University of Oklahoma Press, 1975), p. 164.

14. *Baseball-Reference.com*.

15. Barney Brantingham, *Pro Football Hall of Fame: The Story Behind the Dream*, (Canton, Ohio: Pro Football Hall of Fame, 1990), p. 9.

16. Kristin Wilson, "Basketball prowess still a mystery," *Carlisle Sentinel*, May 12, 2005, <http://www.cumberlink.com/articles/2005/05/12/news/news01.prt> (May 10, 2007).

17. Ibid.

18. "Jim Thorpe Ticket," *History Detectives*, © 2003–2008 <http://www.pbs.org/opb/historydetectives/investigations/310_thorpe.html> (October 29, 2006).

19. Wheeler, p. 192.

20. Personal interview with Grace Thorpe, May 14, 2007.

CHAPTER 8
"Jim Sits With Me"

1. Gene Schoor, *The Jim Thorpe Story: America's Greatest Athlete* (New York: Pocket Books, 1972), p. 166.
2. International Olympic Committee, "Los Angeles, 1932, Games of the X Olympiad," <http://www.olympic.org/uk/games/past/index_uk.asp?OLGT=1&OLGY=1932> (March 15, 2008).
3. Robert W. Wheeler, *Jim Thorpe: World's Greatest Athlete* (Norman, Okla.: University of Oklahoma Press, 1975), p. 196.
4. Ibid.
5. Personal interview with Grace Thorpe, May 14, 2007.
6. Ibid.
7. Ibid.
8. Wheeler, p. 201; personal interview with Grace Thorpe, May 14, 2007.
9. Personal interview with Jack Thorpe, March 17, 2008.
10. Ibid.
11. The Associated Press and Grolier, *Pursuit of Excellence: The Olympic Story* (Danbury, Conn.: Grolier Enterprises, Inc., 1979), p. 68.
12. Personal interview with Grace Thorpe, May 14, 2007.
13. Ibid.
14. Wheeler, p. 217.
15. Ibid., p. 222.
16. Personal interview with Grace Thorpe, May 14, 2007.
17. Personal interview with Jack Thorpe, March 17, 2008.

CHAPTER 9
Officially the Greatest

1. *Jim Thorpe: World's Greatest Athlete*, Official Site of Jim Thorpe, n.d., <http://www.cmgworldwide.com/sports/thorpe/quotes.htm> (October 29, 2006).

GLOSSARY

All-American—Officially chosen by experts as the best in a specific amateur sport.

antibiotics—Medicines that can destroy diseases.

coed—An activity or a school open to both genders; also a female college student.

eligibility—In college sports, permitted to officially play on a varsity team.

farm team—A team that is part of a major league team's minor league system, in which inexperienced players can learn to strengthen their playing ability.

forward pass—In football, a pass thrown usually by the quarterback from behind the line of scrimmage toward the opposing team's goal line.

fumble—To drop the football while a play is in session.

Great Depression—A period in history, ranging through most of the 1930s, in which the state of the economy was poor; best known for massive rates of unemployment.

gridiron—The football field, named because of its resemblance to a cooking utensil called a gridiron.

javelin—A spear a little over eight feet long thrown for distance in track meets.

line of scrimmage—The spot on a football field where the football is placed before the start of a new play.

semipro—Taking part in a sport and getting paid for it, but not as a full-time profession.

shot put—A heavy metal ball pushed or heaved, rather than thrown, for distance in track meets.

slider—In baseball, a pitch that curves downward and sideward and is faster than a curveball.

stereotype—To prejudge people based on preconceived ideas; also a person who is stereotyped.

thrown for a loss—In football, to lose yardage especially when the ball carrier is tackled behind the line of scrimmage.

FURTHER READING

Brown, Don. *Bright Path: Young Jim Thorpe*. New Milford, Conn.: Roaring Brook Press, 2006.

Bruchac, Joseph. *Jim Thorpe: Original All-American*. New York: Dial Books, 2006.

Cook, Sally and James Charlton. *Hey Batta Batta Swing!: The Wild Old Days of Baseball*. New York: M.K. McElderry Books, 2007.

Kalman, Bobbie. *Field Events in Action*. New York: Crabtree Pub., 2005.

Madden, John with Bill Gutman. *John Madden's Heroes of Football: The Story of America's Game*. New York: Dutton Childrens Book, 2006.

Middleton, Haydn. *Modern Olympic Games*. Chicago: Heinemann Library, 2008.

Schilling, Vincent. *Great Athletes from Our First Nations*. Toronto: Second Story Press, 2007.

——*Native Athletes in Action!* Summertown, Tenn.: 7th Generation, 2007.

Smithsonian Institution. *Baseball!: Q & A*. New York: HarperCollins, 2007.

Wingate, Brian. *Football: Rules, Tips, Strategy, and Safety*. New York: Rosen Pub. Group, Inc., 2007.

INTERNET ADDRESSES

Jim Thorpe Association

<http://www.jimthorpeassoc.org/>

The official site for the Jim Thorpe Association.

Jim Thorpe: "The Greatest Athlete in the World"

**<http://www.olympic.org/uk/athletes/profiles/
bio_uk.asp?PAR_I_ID=54230>**

*This International Olympic Committee Web site provides
an overview of Thorpe's involvement in the 1912
Olympics as well as some stunning photos from the
track and field events.*

Official Web Site for Jim Thorpe

<http://www.cmgww.com/sports/thorpe/>

This site has detailed information on Thorpe.

INDEX